MO-MENTUM PRINCIPLES

STAYING BALANCED & MOVING FORWARD

MO-MENTUM PRINCIPLES

STAYING BALANCED & MOVING FORWARD

by

Delton de Armas

ICNU PRESS

Ocala, Florida

FIRST EDITION

Published by ICNU Press

Ocala, Florida

Printed in the United States of America

ISBN: 979-8-9925629-2-7

Imprint: ICNU Press

DEDICATION

To Nestor

For sharing your sage counsel and shrewd understanding as we rode to the tops of mountains (and as I chased you down).

I love and miss you much!

TABLE OF CONTENTS

PREFACE   1

THE START   3

FINDING YOUR BALANCE   11

READING THE TRAIL   29

THE FLOW   47

RIGHT GEAR, RIGHT TIME   71

THE LONG CLIMB   85

WEATHERING THE STORM   103

THE SCENIC ROUTE   117

THE RETURN JOURNEY   129

APPENDIX   143

ACKNOWLEDGEMENTS   157

ABOUT THE AUTHOR   159

PREFACE

I HOLD DEGREES in accounting and finance and spent nearly twenty years as a CFO before moving into consulting. By all traditional measures, I should find financial statements as comfortable as an old riding jersey. Yet I've always felt like something of an outsider in the accounting world. Too creative, too restless, too focused on the why rather than just the how.

That's probably why, after years of interpreting financial statements, especially cash flow, for business owners, I became frustrated with the standard explanations. The technical definitions worked on paper, but they rarely created that "aha moment" entrepreneurs needed. Even with spreadsheets and meticulously documented examples, I saw through the glazed looks and polite nods that signaled a disconnect.

Then one day, while talking through—yet again—the concept of cash flow with a client, I found myself verbally processing. And in the middle of that conversation, something clicked as I heard myself say it out loud: **the cash flow statement is simply looking at the balance sheet change over time.**

That was it. That was the insight that finally unlocked understanding for my client, and, in a way, for me.

How could I make this insight more accessible, more available?

I tried writing a business management book, one that laid everything out clearly and logically. But when I finished, I realized I had written something that was technically accurate but, if I'm honest, about as engaging as a financial audit in the summertime. It captured the mechanics but missed the magic. It lacked authenticity.

That's when my friend Adam—knowing my natural tendency to tell stories—suggested writing a parable. A story to relay the information in a relatable way. It seemed like the perfect way to make the complex simple. And cycling, my lifelong passion, offered the perfect metaphor.

On a bike, financial concepts suddenly made sense. Cash flow became momentum. Balance sheets became terrain. P&Ls became effort over distance. The abstract became tangible, something you could feel in your legs and lungs rather than just calculate in a spreadsheet.

I owe many of my financial and life lessons to my uncle Nestor, a CPA and CFO himself. He had a gift for asking simple questions that revealed deeper truths. Though our conversations often happened on the ski slopes instead of bicycle trails, his way of making complex ideas accessible through everyday experience inspired the (very fictional) Uncle Mo in these pages.

So this book is for anyone who has ever looked at a financial statement and thought, *There must be a clearer way to understand this.* For the entrepreneurs and business owners who know they need financial literacy but can't quite connect with traditional explanations. And even for CPAs and finance professionals who, like me, have struggled to explain technical concepts in a way their clients can grasp.

Through Greg's rides with Uncle Mo, I hope you'll discover what I've learned over the years: that financial understanding isn't about memorizing rules or formulas; it's about seeing patterns, building momentum, and knowing when to shift gears.

Let's ride.

—Delton

THE START

GREG'S FATHER HANDLED numbers for a living. He spoke of them at dinner with the same steady cadence he used for everything else in life. The clatter of silverware punctuated his lectures.

"Spend less than you earn and do it for a long time. That's the secret to getting rich," he'd say, fork suspended over his picadillo, waiting for Greg to acknowledge the wisdom.

Greg nodded at appropriate intervals, but the lessons never stuck. Numbers on paper meant nothing to him. He needed motion. Momentum. Something tangible.

What his father saw as simple math, Greg experienced as a kind of quiet pressure, an expectation to fall in line, to do the sensible thing, to stay within the safe bounds of spreadsheets and savings accounts. But Greg's restlessness didn't balance neatly like a ledger. It pulsed in his chest. It kept him awake at night, sketching out half-baked business ideas on the back of junk mail.

Greg tried to care. He really did. He tracked expenses, set goals, even built a budget once. But it always felt like pedaling a bike with the brakes half on. No matter how hard he worked, he never felt like he was getting anywhere.

What his father saw as stability, Greg experienced as stagnation. He didn't want to manage life. He wanted to move. To build something. To feel wind in his face, not numbers in a column.

That's why he called Uncle Mo.

Mo eagerly agreed when Greg asked to chat but insisted on being eyeball-to-eyeball. Not surprising. Mo's warmth always came across on the phone, but nothing compared to being in the room with him. This was especially true when conversations carried weight.

Greg had called to ask about the mowing business he was starting. Mo, sensing the weight behind his words, invited him over.

Greg swung his leg over his trusted steel stallion and pedaled toward Uncle Mo's, hoping the conversation would bring some clarity, or at least a jolt of energy. As he rode, he imagined how the conversation might go. But deep down, he knew it wouldn't follow the script. It never did with Mo.

Moisés "Mo" Morales stood about even with Greg at five-nine, but with a clean bald head that caught the light. Not that height mattered; Mo filled whatever space he occupied. Something about his presence made ordinary moments spark with possibility. He also had a way of making you feel like you were the most important person in the room.

"Greggo!" Mo's voice boomed across the driveway when Greg pulled up. "Perfect timing!"

Greg smiled before he even looked up. Just hearing Mo's voice confirmed he'd made the right call.

The garage door stood open, tools arranged with deliberate disorder across a workbench. Mo emerged wiping grease from his hands with a red shop rag that had seen better decades.

"You still riding that hand-me-down Schwinn?" Mo asked, nodding toward Greg's bike leaning against the fence.

"Gets me where I need to go."

"That's what your father would say." Mo tossed the rag onto the bench. "But is it the ride you want?"

Greg shrugged. Classic Mo, never asking simple questions.

"Come on in," Mo said, "I need another set of hands."

Inside, a vintage *Look* road bike with Team Kelme branding and a blue and yellow frame hung from hooks on the wall, its rear wheel removed and mounted on a strange metal contraption with calibrated gauges.

"Truing stand," Mo explained, catching Greg's curious look. "This wheel's wobbling like a drunk guy in a hula-hoop contest." He handed Greg a small metal tool. "Know how to use a spoke wrench?"

Greg shook his head.

"Perfect opportunity to learn. This is always easier with two people." Mo positioned himself behind the stand. "I'll spin the wheel; you'll adjust the spokes where I tell you. Clockwise tightens, counterclockwise loosens. Quarter turns only."

He spun the wheel, eyes narrowed at a specific point where the rim passed the gauge. "There," he said, pointing, "three spokes to your left, tighten a quarter turn."

Greg fumbled slightly with the wrench, finding the right spoke.

"Good. Now the next one over, same thing." Mo continued spinning, calling out adjustments. "See how it works? The wheel tells us what it needs if we know how to listen."

As they worked together, the rhythm became smoother, Mo spinning and pointing, Greg adjusting with increasing confidence. The wobble gradually disappeared.

"Two minds, four hands," Mo said, "problems solve themselves faster." Mo smiled with satisfaction as the wheel spun true. The garage smelled of possibility, and GT-85 lubricant.

Mo grabbed the wheel of the stand and positioned himself beneath the bike hanging behind them to reinstall it.

"So," Mo said, his voice echoing slightly. "You're finally doing it."

Greg leaned against the workbench. "Yeah. Been thinking about it for a while."

"Thinking doesn't cut grass." Mo grunted, tightening something beneath the bicycle. "What pushed you over the edge?"

"Tired of working for other people, I guess."

Mo stopped and looked at Greg from under the bike frame. "Weak."

"What?"

"That's a weak reason to start something hard." He resumed working. "Try again."

Greg frowned. "Fine. I want to build something that's mine. Something I control."

"Better." A metallic ping sounded as something small dropped from the bike to the concrete floor. Mo ignored it. "But still not enough."

Greg's frustration flared. "Look, do you want the real answer or the one that sounds good?"

"Ah!" Mo emerged, pointing the wrench at Greg. "Now we're getting somewhere."

Greg looked away, suddenly aware of how badly he wanted Mo's approval. "I don't know what I'm doing with my life. Everyone else seems to have it figured out. I thought maybe if I built something…"

"You'd figure yourself out along the way?" Mo set the wrench down. "Not bad, kid. There's truth in that."

Mo wiped his hands again and pulled two bottles of water from a small fridge in the corner. He tossed one to Greg.

"So what's the plan?" Mo asked.

"Simple. Mow lawns. Make money."

Mo's laugh filled the garage. "Simple! He says it's simple!" He unscrewed his water bottle. "Tell me, what happens when Mrs. Rodriguez wants her lawn mowed, but can't pay you for three weeks?"

Greg opened his mouth, then closed it.

"Or when your mower breaks, you need $300 for parts, but your next paycheck from existing clients won't cover it?"

"I'd…"

"Or when you land your first big contract that pays double your usual rate, but requires you to hire help first?"

Greg stared, his water untouched.

"That's cash flow, Greggo." Mo took a long drink. "And ignoring it kills more small businesses than anything else."

"Dad never mentioned cash flow. Just budgeting and saving."

"Your dad draws a salary. Different world." Mo gestured around the garage. "Out here, timing matters more than total. You can make a million dollars on paper and still go bankrupt waiting for the money to arrive."

Greg's stomach tightened. He hadn't considered this.

"Look." Mo grabbed a worn notebook from the workbench. "This isn't complicated, but it requires attention. You track what comes in, what goes out, and most importantly, *when* it happens."

He flipped it open to reveal columns of numbers, dates, and notes.

"This was my first business. Bicycle repair, before I built my landscaping company."

Greg stepped closer, suddenly interested. Mo rarely talked about his early days.

"See this?" Mo pointed to a series of entries. "June 1998. I had three major repairs due, parts already ordered. Then my supplier doubled their minimum order requirement without warning. I had the clients, had the skills, but didn't have the cash to front the parts."

"What'd you do?"

Mo tapped the page. "Called every client personally. Offered a ten percent discount if they'd pay half upfront instead of the usual pay-on-completion."

"Did it work?"

"Two said yes. One went elsewhere." Mo shrugged. "I lost some profit margin but kept the business alive. That's the game."

He closed the notebook and handed it to Greg.

"Start here. Track everything. Even the small stuff."

Greg took the notebook, surprised by how worn the cover felt. "Is this…"

"My original? Yeah. Consider it your first business asset."

Greg looked up, caught off guard by the gesture.

Mo cleared his throat. "First lesson in there: figure out how long you can go without getting paid. Your 'runway,' so to speak. Most people think too much about profit and not enough about timing."

He stood and grabbed his bike helmet from a hook.

"Second lesson: let's go for a ride."

"Now? I thought we were talking business."

Mo was already wheeling his bike outside. "We are. But some things you need to feel, not just hear. Bring your Schwinn."

Greg tucked the notebook into his back pocket and followed, squinting in the sunlight. By the time he got his bike upright, Mo was already pedaling down the street.

"First stop," Mo called over his shoulder, "the hill on Prospect Avenue. I want you to experience something!"

Greg pushed off, legs pumping to catch up. The notebook pressed against him with each pedal stroke, a small weight that somehow felt significant.

Whatever lesson Mo had planned, Greg knew one thing for sure: he'd never look at his father's dinner table lectures the same way again. This—the wind in his face, the pursuit of something unknown—this he could understand.

FINDING YOUR BALANCE

GREG'S LUNGS BURNED by the time they reached the base of Prospect Avenue. Mo hadn't even broken a sweat.

"This hill," Mo said, nodding toward the incline, "has taught me more about business than most books."

Greg leaned over his handlebars, trying—and failing—to catch his breath. "Hard." He took a breath between his words. "To see how."

Mo ignored the comment. "Before we climb, let me ask you something." He dismounted. "Still have that notebook I gave you?" Greg fumbled around in his back pocket and pulled it out for Mo to see, a pen cradled in the crease. "Good. Find a blank page and write down everything you think you'll spend money on in your first month of business."

Greg took the notebook, still breathing hard. "Now?"

"Now."

Greg scribbled a quick list:

☐ Gas for mower
☐ Equipment maintenance
☐ Business cards
☐ Maybe a website?

He handed it back to Mo, who glanced at it and frowned.

"You're missing at least twelve things."

"Twelve? No way."

Mo motioned toward himself with his hand, his empty fingers cradling an invisible writing instrument. Greg handed him his pen. "Insurance." He wrote it down. "Transportation costs." Another note. "Taxes. Equipment depreciation. Banking fees. Phone service for taking calls. Work clothes. Blade sharpening. Waste disposal. Accounting software. Emergency repairs. Marketing beyond just cards."

Greg stared at the expanded list. "I was only going to charge fifteen bucks a lawn."

"And now you know why most lawn businesses start in the Spring and fail before August." Mo handed the pen and notebook back to Greg. "That right there? That's the start of your Profit and Loss statement. P&L for short."

Greg remembered his father mentioning P&Ls during dinner. "Dad talked about those sometimes."

"And I bet your eyes glazed over."

Greg couldn't argue with that. "Seems like he called it something else. Income statement, maybe?"

"Same thing. Different name." Mo clearly understood his confusion. "It's been called a lot of things by a lot of people. Statement of Earnings, or Earnings Statement. Statement of Operations, or Operating Statement. Even Revenue and Expense Statement."

"Oh. So those are all talking about the same thing?" Greg was genuinely curious, and his confusion was beginning to fade.

"Whatever you choose to call it," Mo responded, "it's a summary of your income, of what you've earned—revenue—and what you've spent—expenses. Subtract your expenses from your revenue, and you've got your net income. That's an oversimplification, but I'm sure you get it."

"I'm starting to," Greg admitted.

Mo straddled his bike again. "Let's ride. We're going to climb this hill twice. First time, use only one gear. No shifting. Second time, shift whenever you need to."

"What's this got to do with P&L statements?"

"Everything." Mo pushed off. "Come on!"

The slope looked steeper the closer they got. Mo pedaled steadily ahead while Greg struggled to match his pace in a fixed gear. Halfway up, Greg's legs screamed in protest. Three-quarters of the way, he had to dismount and walk, pushing his bike alongside.

Mo waited at the top, barely winded.

"That," he said when Greg finally arrived, "is what happens when you run a business without understanding your P&L. *Trabajar el doble por no trabajar.* You work twice as hard to try to avoid working."

Greg wiped sweat from his forehead. "I couldn't maintain speed."

"You couldn't maintain speed because the gear you were in was too hard to push uphill. Now we're going back down and then back up again. This time though, on the way up, shift gears whenever you need to."

The descent gave Greg a moment to recover. At the bottom, Mo waited.

"Ready? Pay attention to how it feels, and shift as you need to."

They began the climb again. This time, Greg shifted down when the incline steepened, keeping his pedaling consistent and manageable. When the inclined eased, he shifted again to keep his cadence. He still worked hard but reached the top without stopping. He kept a much faster pace, too, arriving just seconds after Mo.

"Better?" Mo asked.

"Much!" Greg seemed surprised by the difference.

"That's your P&L in action. When you understand what you're spending versus what you're bringing in, you can shift before you stall out." Mo gestured toward a bench overlooking the neighborhood. "Two times up Prospect deserves a little break."

Greg couldn't contain his excitement. For the first time, financial statements felt like something real, something useful, not just paperwork his father droned on about. "I get it now," he said, almost to himself. "It's not just numbers on a page; it's like having gauges on a dashboard. You can actually see what's happening and adjust."

Mo's eyes crinkled with amusement. "Look at you. I think we've got a convert."

They sat, bikes leaning against the back of the bench. The town spread out below them. Houses, businesses, parks. From up here, everything looked connected.

"The key to the P&L," Mo said, "is understanding that it covers a period of time. A month, a quarter, a year. It's not a snapshot; it's a story."

"What kind of story?"

"The story of how your money moved. Where it came from, where it went." Mo pulled out his water bottle. "Most small business owners only look at the bottom line. Did I make money or lose money? But the real intelligence is in the details."

Greg thought about the list they'd made. "So I need to track everything."

"Everything." Mo took a long drink. "But tracking isn't enough. You need to understand how the parts relate to each other."

He reached into his pocket and pulled out a folded piece of paper, smoothing it on his knee.

"This was my P&L from my first year in business. See these categories? Revenue at the top. That's all the money coming in. Then expenses below, everything going out. The difference is your profit or loss."

Greg studied the paper. The columns looked familiar from his father's explanations but somehow seeing them filled with real numbers made them more interesting.

"Why are some expenses grouped together?"

"Good eye." Mo tapped the paper. "Fixed costs versus variable costs. Fixed stay roughly the same no matter how many lawns you mow. Insurance, for example. Variable costs change with volume. More lawns equal more gas used."

Greg noticed something else. "You've got notes in the margins."

"The numbers tell you what happened. The notes tell you why." Mo pointed to one section. "See here? Revenue dropped in September. My note explains that we had three weeks of rain. The next month shows higher maintenance costs because all the equipment needed servicing after sitting idle."

For the first time, Greg could see how a P&L might actually be useful.

"So it's not just for taxes."

Mo laughed. "Ummm…no. It's your business dashboard. Tells you if you need to raise prices, cut costs, or find more clients."

Greg looked across the town below. Hundreds of lawns stretched out in neat rectangles.

"I never thought about the rain affecting business."

"Right. The P&L forces you to connect events with outcomes." Mo folded the paper. "Your dad's job has a predictable paycheck. Out here, you need to understand the patterns."

Mo stood up. "But here's what they don't teach you in accounting class. The P&L can lie to you."

"What? How?"

"It shows you earned $5,000 this month but doesn't tell you that $3,000 of it hasn't been paid yet." Mo grabbed his bike. "That's why cash flow matters more than profit, especially when you're starting out."

Greg thought about this as they began riding again, this time along the ridge that followed the top of the hill.

"So I could look profitable on paper but have no money in the bank?"

"Now you're getting it." Mo veered onto a path that cut through a small wooded area. "I knew a landscaper who landed a contract with the city. Looked great on his P&L. Doubled his revenue overnight. Six months later, he was out of business."

"What happened?"

"City paid on a ninety-day cycle. He had to front all the costs—labor, materials, equipment—but didn't get paid for three months. His P&L showed a healthy business, but his bank account told the truth."

The path opened into a clearing where several trails converged. Mo stopped.

"Here's another lesson. Notice how all these paths connect? Your P&L connects to your other financial statements. It doesn't exist in isolation."

Greg stopped beside him. "Other statements?"

"Your Balance Sheet and Cash Flow Statement. We'll get to those." Mo checked his watch. "But first, let's get practical. When we get back, I want you to draft your projected P&L for your first three months."

"I don't have any real numbers yet."

"So estimate. Better to be prepared with an imperfect plan than perfectly unprepared."

They turned and headed back toward Mo's house, taking a different trail that wound gradually downhill. The ride back was easier, giving Greg time to think.

"You know," Mo said as they coasted, "your dad's not wrong about saving. But for a business owner, saving takes on a different meaning."

"How so?"

"It's not just about putting money aside for retirement. It's about creating reserves to smooth out the bumps." Mo turned to look at Greg. "Those three weeks of rain I mentioned? I survived because I had two months of expenses saved."

The trail emptied onto a residential street. They rode the final blocks to Mo's house in silence.

Back in the garage, Mo hung his bike and pulled two chairs up to the workbench.

"Alright, let's draft that P&L." He cleared a space and laid out a blank sheet of paper. "Start with your revenue projections. How many lawns can you realistically mow in a week?"

Greg thought about it. "Maybe fifteen to start? Working after my regular job and weekends."

"And your price point?"

"I was thinking fifteen dollars per lawn, but after seeing that expense list…"

"Let's work backwards," Mo said, flipping open his notebook. "What you charge should come *after* you understand your numbers. But you have to start somewhere. So let's start with fifteen a yard and test it."

Greg gave a half-nod as Mo wrote in his notebook.

He drew a few columns across the top of the page. "First, let's look at your variable costs, stuff that goes up the more lawns you mow. What's gas cost you?"

"About six bucks to fill the tank. I usually get two yards per tank."

"So, three bucks per yard just for fuel." Mo wrote it down. "What else?"

"I take the blade in for sharpening once a week, about every fifteen lawns. They charge fourteen bucks, so… I guess that's, what, about a dollar a yard?"

Mo nodded. "Keep going."

"I'll need to replace the spark plug, air filter, oil, that kind of stuff. Hard to say how often, but maybe fifty bucks every couple of months?"

"So, $25 a month divided by how many lawns?"

"If I do fifteen a week, that's sixty a month… call it forty cents a yard."

Mo totaled the column. "So you're at $4.40 in variable costs per yard."

Greg frowned. "That seems high."

"It adds up faster than people think." Mo tapped the page. "So let's see where you stand."

60 lawns × $15 = $900 revenue

60 lawns × $4.40 = $264 variable costs

Profit = $636

"Now let's look at your fixed costs. What'll you owe each month no matter how many lawns you mow? You know, for general stuff."

Greg pondered that for a second, then ran through the list. "I think insurance is like $75. Ads and flyers, maybe $125. A phone plan, I think another $50 or so?"

Insurance – $75

Ads and flyers – $125

Phone plan – $50

Mo jotted it down. "So we'll call it $250 a month in fixed costs."

He slid the notebook toward Greg. "Let's plug it in."

Scenario A: Charging $15 per yard

Revenue	$900
Variable costs	$264
Gross Profit	$636
Fixed costs	$250
Net Profit	$386

Greg raised an eyebrow. "That's not bad."

"Hang on," Mo said. "That's your profit, not your paycheck. And you're the one mowing, right?"

"Yeah."

"How much do you want to pay yourself per lawn?"

Greg thought for a second. "Ten bucks?"

Mo raised an eyebrow. "So $600 a month in labor. Where's that coming from?"

Greg scanned the page again. "That wipes out everything."

"Exactly," Mo said, pointing to the net profit. "If you pay yourself like an employee, there's nothing left for the business. No buffer. No savings. No reinvestment."

He flipped the page and ran the same math at $22.

$$60 \text{ lawns} \times \$22 = \$1320 \text{ revenue}$$

$$60 \text{ lawns} \times \$4.40 = \$264 \text{ variable costs}$$

$$\text{Gross Profit} = \$1056$$

"Watch what bumping your price a little does to the P&L."

Scenario B: Charging $22 per yard

Revenue	$1329
Variable costs	$264
Gross Profit	$1056
Fixed costs	$250
Net Profit	$806
Pay Yourself	$600
Leftover	$206

"Now you've got room to breathe. Let's call that leftover piece *business profit*. For now, plan on setting that aside, so you can reinvest it into your business. If anything goes wrong—equipment breaks, weather slows you down, whatever—you're not underwater."

Greg exhaled slowly.

"One more," Mo said, already writing.

Scenario C: Charging $25 per yard

60 lawns × $25 = $1500 revenue

60 lawns × $4.40 = $264 variable costs

Gross Profit = $1236

"That's a pretty strong gross margin," Mo said as he wrote. "Now watch this. I'm going to change the P&L a little. Since you're paying yourself as an employee, and you're getting paid $10 per yard, let's treat that as a variable expense and include it above the gross profit line. We'll call all those variable costs your 'Cost of Sales.' It's the costs you incur so that you can have revenue."

Scenario C: Charging $25 per yard

Revenue	$1500
Cost of Sales	$864
Gross Profit	$636

"The costs I incur so I can make sales. The *cost*-of-*sales*. That makes sense!"

"Then, let's call those fixed costs we came up with 'General and administrative expenses, or G-and-A.'"

Gross Profit	$636
G&A expenses	$250
Net Profit	$386

21

Mo, stating what was becoming obvious to Greg, remarked, "Same work. Same effort. But a better cushion and a stronger business."

Greg stared at the numbers, quiet for a beat. Then he grinned. "Fifteen a yard suddenly feels a little cheap."

Mo chuckled. "Fifteen is how you stay busy. Twenty-five is how you stay in business."

Greg stared at the number. "That's higher than I first thought, but seeing how it plays out, it makes a lot more sense."

"Most people undercharge because they don't account for all their costs." Mo started writing again. "But now let me show you something interesting, and quite useful. Let's take that net profit, and see how much you're making, net, per yard. How would you do that?

"You would just divide that profit by the number of yards, right?"

"Right. It's not hard, but I just wanted to make sure you were tracking with me. So $386 divided by 60 yards is $6.43 per yard. Let's just call that $6, to keep things simple. Now, watch what happens when we reduce your price per yard by $6.

Scenario D: Charging $19 per yard

Revenue	$1140
Cost of Sales	$864
Gross Profit	$276
G&A expenses	$250
Net Profit	$26

"That $26 is rounding. If we'd used our computed number of $6.43 to reduce sales, your net profit would've been $0. In other words, you would have *broken even*. So, your breakeven price per yard is $19, or more precisely, $18.57."

"So that's my bare minimum."

"Right. We call this a breakeven analysis. Your breakeven tells you the minimum price you need to charge for survival. Below this, you're paying people to mow their lawns."

Greg's forehead wrinkled. "I like cutting grass well enough, I guess, but not enough to pay people to let me do it!"

"Now you're getting it. Breakeven analysis can be a powerful tool. Our example was pretty simple, but when you're forecasting, it can get more complicated. Think about it. There are a lot of moving parts in your P&L, and they could all affect your breakeven."

"I think I understand," Greg said in a sort of whisper. "If I only had 14 yards per week, that would be 56 for the month, so my revenue would be lower."

"Right," Mo affirmed, seeing Greg's wheels turn. "But what else would be lower?"

"My variable costs. I would have fewer lawns, so my total variable costs would go down because while the costs per lawn are the same, when you multiply that by a smaller number of yards, the total is smaller."

"Great insight, and I'm glad you brought that up. Your variable costs are actually fixed per yard."

"Ahhh. That's right. And a little surprising when you say it like that. My variable costs are a fixed amount per yard. Wait a minute, that means my fixed costs are variable per yard! I mean, they are, right?"

"Yep! You got there quick, Greggo! It sounds backwards, I know, but you have fixed—that is, unchanging—costs for every

23

yard you mow, but they vary based on the number of yards. Then you have costs that are the same. They don't vary, no matter how many yards you mow. So if you change how many yards you mow in a given month, that changes the denominator of the fraction: fixed costs over yards mowed. So your fixed costs are actually variable per yard."

Greg's head was spinning, but it was starting to click. "Variable costs are fixed…per yard. And my fixed costs are variable…per yard. Sheesh. That could be confusing!"

"Confusing, yes. But not hard. But the number of variables and the variety of impacts they can have on the P&L adds complexity to your analysis."

"I see. That's what you meant when you said a breakeven analysis can get complicated. There can be so many different scenarios."

"We call that scenario analysis." Mo smiled in admiration of Greg's progress. "But we're getting ahead of ourselves. For now, I think it's enough to know how to compute your breakeven point."

"That way, if I have to discount my prices for some reason, I know how far I can go before I'm paying people to let me mow."

While Greg's face shown bright with understanding, the garage had grown dimmer as evening approached. Mo turned on the workbench light, casting long shadows behind them.

"There's something else I want to show you." He reached under the bench and pulled out an old, dusty box. Inside was a stack of papers—old financial statements, by the look of them.

"This was my first proper business. Bike repair shop downtown, before I built my landscaping company." Mo spread several sheets on the bench. "Look at the P&L for the first year. What do you notice?"

Greg studied the numbers, surprised to see red ink. "You lost money."

"The first eight months, yes." Mo pointed to the ninth month. "Then something changed. See the jump in revenue?"

The numbers nearly doubled.

"What happened?"

Mo smiled. "Tour de France, 1986."

Greg looked at him blankly.

"Greg LeMond won. First American ever." Mo's voice held a hint of something Greg couldn't place. "Suddenly everyone wanted road bikes. Repairs, upgrades, new purchases."

"Lucky timing."

"Was it?" Mo flipped to another sheet. "Look at the expenses in the months before. Marketing doubled. New specialty tools. Training courses in high-end road bike mechanics."

Greg looked closer. "You were preparing."

"I saw an opportunity coming and positioned myself to catch it. That's what your P&L can tell you, where to invest ahead of trends." Mo gathered the papers.

Mo continued, "But you know what's not in these numbers? The sixteen-hour days. The doubts. The customers who thought I was crazy to specialize when mountain bikes were the trend."

He closed the box and slid it back under the bench.

"The P&L shows results, not effort. Remember that when things get tough."

Greg's eyebrows rose in recognition, a new respect blooming for his uncle.

"Make a copy of this," Mo said, pushing the projected P&L toward Greg. "Update it weekly with real numbers as you get started. After three months, we'll compare what happened versus what you projected."

Greg carefully folded the paper. "Thanks, Uncle Mo. This is… clearer than I expected."

"The principle is simple. Execution is hard." Mo stood and stretched. "Next time, we'll talk about your Balance Sheet. It's like reading the trail ahead, knowing what's coming before you get there."

Greg tucked the P&L into the notebook Mo had given him. "I still need to get my first client."

"Start with Mrs. Abernathy next door to your parents. Her regular service just raised prices, and her arthritis is getting worse." Mo winked. "Tell her I sent you."

Greg raised an eyebrow. "You've been thinking about this."

"I think about a lot of things." Mo opened the refrigerator and pulled out two sodas. "Most people see business as complicated. Really, it's just paying attention to the right details at the right time." He handed a can to Greg. "Just like riding."

They stepped outside into the early evening. The temperature had dropped, bringing a coolness that hinted at approaching autumn.

"One last thing," Mo said, popping open his soda. "LeMond didn't win that Tour because he was the strongest rider."

"No?"

"He won because he knew exactly how much energy he had left and when to spend it." Mo took a drink. "Your P&L does the same thing. It tells you what resources you have and where best to use them."

As Greg rode home later, the notebook secure in his backpack, he found himself looking at the lawns he passed differently. Not just grass to be cut, but opportunities with costs, variables, and potential. The P&L in his bag wasn't just a sheet of paper with estimates; it was the beginning of seeing his world through new eyes.

READING THE TRAIL

SATURDAY MORNING ARRIVED with the smell of fresh coffee with a splash of opportunity. Greg had spent the week securing his first three lawn clients. Mrs. Abernathy as Mo suggested, plus the Wilsons down the street and Mr. Chen who lived on the corner. Twenty-five dollars per lawn, paid upfront. Mo would be proud.

Greg always got up early, even on Saturdays. The notebook sat open on Greg's kitchen table, each page gradually filling with notes, numbers, and questions. He'd been diligent about tracking expenses, even the small ones, like gas for his car to drive to clients, a new blade for his mower, business cards printed at the local shop.

His dad, an early riser himself, walked in to make his morning *cafecito*. As he added grounds from the yellow can of Café Bustelo to the base of his *cafetera*, he greeted Greg. "*Buenos días, mijo.*"

"Mornin', Dad." He didn't even look up, engrossed in the pages before him.

"What's got you so engrossed this early on a Saturday?"

Greg hoped his dad wasn't baiting him, but he answered anyway. "I'm trying to get a sense of how my lawn business is doing. Uncle Mo is helping me understand the financial statements."

"Uncle Mo is helping you with financial statements? Hmph. I bet I can guess how that's going for ya."

"What do you mean? I've been learning a lot from him!"

"That's like learning double-entry bookkeeping from someone who counts on his fingers."

Greg rolled his eyes at the sarcasm, but not where his dad could see. He meant no disrespect, but he'd grown weary of Dad's jabs at Mo. He knew that's just how brothers acted sometimes, but he certainly didn't want to get in the middle of it. Especially since his uncle had recently taken an interest in helping him.

His thoughts snapped back to reality when his phone buzzed with a text from Mo: *Meet at Riverview Trail. 7 a.m. Bring bike and notebook.*

Greg smiled. Another lesson wrapped in a ride.

The morning air carried a hint of autumn crispness when Greg pulled into the trailhead parking lot. Mo was already there, leaning against his truck, two paper cups in hand, steam wafting from the *cortaditos* he'd brought for them.

"Morning, Greggo." Mo extended one of the cups. "Figured you'd need this."

"Thanks." Greg took a grateful sip. "Three clients so far."

Mo's eyebrows lifted. "And you're charging...?"

"Twenty-five each. Paid before I cut."

Mo's approval beamed in his expression. "Smart. How's the tracking going?"

Greg patted his backpack. "Every penny, just like you said."

"Good man." Mo set his coffee on the truck's tailgate and began unloading his bike. "Today we're talking Balance Sheets. And for that, we need terrain."

Riverview Trail was known for its technical sections. Roots, rocks, and sudden elevation changes challenged even experienced riders. Greg hadn't been here in years, not since he'd taken a bad fall and damaged his old mountain bike.

"I'm not sure my Schwinn is up for this," Greg said, eyeing the trail entrance.

Mo motioned at his truck with a slight head nod and a sort of puckering of his lips, almost like he was pointing with his mouth. Greg smirked at the almost humorous gesture. He'd seen his dad do the same thing countless times before.

"Use my spare. It's adjusted for your height already."

Greg caught the lock keys, surprised. Mo's spare bike was a high-end trail model worth more than Greg made last year. "You sure?"

"Can't teach today's lesson on subpar equipment." Mo secured his helmet. "Besides, I trust you."

Something about those three words made Greg stand taller.

They set off down the trail, Mo leading at a comfortable pace. The first section was relatively smooth, allowing them to ride side by side when the path widened.

"So, what do you know about Balance Sheets?" Mo asked.

Greg thought back to his father's dinner table lectures. "Assets, liabilities, and equity. Shows what you own and owe at a specific point in time."

"Own and owe," Mo echoed. "Not bad. But a bit of textbook answer." Mo navigated around a rock. "So what does that *mean*?"

Greg hesitated. "It's… a snapshot of your business?"

"Getting warmer." Mo slowed as the trail narrowed. "The P&L we talked about last time? That's like a video, showing movement over time. The Balance Sheet is the pause button. One precise moment, frozen."

They rounded a bend, and Mo stopped suddenly. He pointed ahead.

"Look at the trail. What do you see?"

Greg surveyed the path. Rocks jutted from the soil at awkward angles. A fallen log bisected the trail. Beyond that, the path narrowed between two large boulders before dropping away steeply.

"I see obstacles."

"Precisely. And what are you going to do about them?"

Greg considered the terrain. "Plan my line. Figure out where to position myself for each section."

Mo smiled. "That's what a Balance Sheet does. It shows you exactly what you're facing at a given moment. Your resources and your obligations. The strong points and weak points. Your line through the business terrain."

He dismounted and walked to the edge of the technical section.

"Your P&L tells you how fast you're moving. Your Balance Sheet tells you what you're moving through." Mo gestured to the trail. "Let's ride this section, then we'll talk more."

Greg watched as Mo remounted, clipped in, and navigated the obstacles with precision, shifting his weight back for the log, threading between the boulders, and braking gradually on the descent. When it was Greg's turn, he followed the same line, though with less grace. The borrowed bike responded beautifully, absorbing impacts that would have thrown his Schwinn off course.

They regrouped at the bottom of the descent.

"What did you notice?" Mo asked.

Greg caught his breath. "I had to adjust constantly. Weight distribution, braking, pedal position. Everything mattered."

"That's business." Mo took a drink from his water bottle. "Your Balance Sheet tells you where your weight is distributed. Too much debt? You'll topple forward. Not enough liquid assets? You can't absorb impacts."

They continued down the trail, settling into a rhythm.

"Let me ask you something," Mo said after a while. "What happens if you spend all your cash buying a fancy new mower?"

"I'd have a great mower but no money."

"And on your Balance Sheet?"

Greg thought about it. "Cash goes down, but equipment value goes up. Assets stay the same, just... different types."

"Bingo!" Mo's voice carried approval. "Total assets don't change, just the composition. This is why the Balance Sheet balances. But what's the danger?"

The trail curved alongside the river, sunlight dappling through the trees.

"If I need cash for something unexpected, I'm stuck."

"Precisely. Asset composition matters as much as total value." Mo led them onto a side trail that climbed gradually up a ridge. "When I was building my landscaping business, I faced a crucial decision. Invest in more equipment or keep cash reserves."

"What did you choose?"

"Both, eventually. But first, I looked at my Balance Sheet." Mo slowed as the incline steepened. "I had decent cash, some equipment, and a small line of credit. But I also saw accounts receivable growing too large."

"Clients not paying?"

"Paying late. Commercial contracts...reliable but slow." Mo stood on his pedals as they climbed. "My Balance Sheet showed me the problem before it became a crisis. I sold some of my unpaid invoices to a financing company for quick cash. Took a small hit on the total but got paid immediately. That kept adequate cash flowing while I expanded equipment."

They reached the ridge top and stopped to rest. The view stretched across the river valley, miles of forest painted in early autumn colors.

"That's a Balance Sheet moment," Mo said, gesturing toward the panorama. "Seeing everything laid out before you. The assets, the liabilities, the path forward."

Greg took out his notebook and pen. "So how do I create one for my business?"

"List everything you own on the left. Cash, equipment, accounts receivable. Everything you owe on the right. Loans, credit cards, accounts payable. The difference is your equity, what's truly yours."

Mo watched as Greg began sketching a simple Balance Sheet format.

"Here's what most people miss," Mo continued. "The Balance Sheet connects directly to your P&L and Cash Flow Statement. They're not separate reports; they're parts of a single story."

Greg looked up. "How so?"

"Remember the net income at the bottom of your P&L? That same number flows into your equity section on the Balance Sheet." Mo took Greg's pen and drew a line connecting the two concepts. "And the cash position on your Balance Sheet? That's where your Cash Flow Statement ends."

"They..." Greg started, pausing as he tried to find the word, *"articulate."* Greg said, recalling a term from his father's explanations.

Mo's eyes lit up. "Exactly! They articulate. They connect and flow into each other mechanically, like a bicycle drivetrain."

He sketched a quick diagram in Greg's notebook. "Think of your P&L as the pedals. That's where the power and motion originate. Your Balance Sheet is like the drivetrain. They transfer and distribute that power. And your Cash Flow Statement is like the rear wheel, where everything ultimately translates into forward movement."

Mo traced the connections on the sketch. "Just as your chain links your pedals and chainring to your rear cassette, your net income links your P&L to your Balance Sheet. And just as the cassette then connects your chain to the wheel, your cash position connects your Balance Sheet to your Cash Flow Statement. When these connections are properly aligned. When they articulate correctly, power flows smoothly through the entire system."

They remounted their bikes and began a section that alternated between short climbs and flowing descents. Mo called back over his shoulder.

"Your father, he's brilliant with numbers. Always was. But he never understood the difference between accounting and finance."

"What's the difference?"

"One looks backwards while the other looks forward." Mo paused, then said it another way. "Accounting tells you what happened. Finance helps you decide what to do next." Mo navigated a tight turn. "Your dad sees balance sheets as compliance documents. I see them as decision tools."

The mention of his father made Greg curious. "Did you and Dad ever work together?"

Mo chuckled. "Once. He helped me set up books for my first business. Kept telling me to focus on tax minimization. I kept asking about growth capital. We drove each other crazy."

35

They emerged from the trees into an open meadow where the trail widened again.

"Your dad and I took different paths," Mo continued. "He chose security and expertise in one area. I wanted to build something from nothing, even with the risks."

They rode in silence for a while, the only sounds the whir of gears and crunch of tires on the trail.

"Let me show you something practical," Mo said eventually. He stopped at a trail intersection. Different colored markings—blue, red, and yellow—were painted on the trees, each indicating a different route. "Choose a path."

Greg surveyed the options. Blue trail continued straight, fairly level. Red trail climbed steeply to the right. Yellow trail descended through what looked like a rock garden.

"What's the lesson here?"

"Choose based on the information you have."

Greg considered. "Blue seems safest."

"Based on what?"

"What I can see from here. Seems flat, straightforward."

Mo had a smirk that peaked out from behind his otherwise serious expression. "That's operating with incomplete information. Now let me show you the trail map." He pulled out his phone and opened a hiking app. "Look at the complete routes."

The map showed that the blue trail eventually ended at a washed-out bridge. Impassable. The red trail, after the initial climb, opened into smooth singletrack that looped back to the parking lot. The yellow trail, while technical, connected to a paved bike path that offered an easy return.

"That's what a complete set of financial statements gives you...the whole map." Mo put his phone away. "Your Balance Sheet tells you where you are right now. Your P&L shows how you got here. Your Cash Flow Statement reveals what's actually moving through the business."

Greg's expression brightened with understanding. "And together they help you choose the right path."

"Yup! That's financial literacy." Mo gestured to the red trail. "Shall we?"

The initial climb was brutal, leaving them both winded. But as promised, it leveled into smooth, flowing trail that wound pleasantly through a pine forest.

"Your Balance Sheet will change constantly," Mo said as they rode. "Every transaction shifts something. Pay a bill; cash goes down, liabilities decrease. Make a sale on credit; accounts receivable go up, equity increases through net income."

"Sounds complicated to track."

"It is and it isn't. Modern accounting software handles the mechanics. Your job is understanding what it means." Mo bunny-hopped over a small root. "Notice how the trail changed? Easier now, but we still need to pay attention."

They emerged from the pines into another clearing. Mo stopped and pulled out a water bottle.

"When you look at your Balance Sheet, there are ratios that tell you how healthy your business is." He took a drink. "Current ratio—current assets divided by current liabilities. Tells you if you can cover short-term obligations."

Greg made a note. "What's a good number?"

"For your business? At least 2:1. Two dollars of current assets for every dollar you owe soon." Mo replaced his water bottle.

"Debt-to-equity ratio shows how much you're borrowing versus what you own. Quick ratio shows if you can pay bills without selling inventory."

"This is getting technical."

"Let's make it practical," Mo suggested. "Pull out your notebook and let's calculate your current ratio right now."

Greg flipped to his latest balance sheet draft.

"Current assets include cash, accounts receivable, and any inventory you have. Things that can be converted to cash within a year," Mo explained. "What's your total?"

Greg added the numbers. "About $3,200. Mostly cash and some receivables from my bi-weekly clients."

"And current liabilities are obligations due within a year. Accounts payable, credit card debt, the portion of any loans due soon. What's your total there?"

Greg calculated. "About $1,400. Mainly the mower payment and some outstanding bills for parts."

"So what's your current ratio?"

Greg divided the numbers. "$3,200 divided by $1,400 is about 2.3 to 1."

"That's healthy," Mo's approval evident in his tone. "Now imagine you lost your two biggest clients tomorrow. How would that change things?"

Greg recalculated, subtracting the receivables from those clients. "It would drop to about 1.8 to 1."

"Still above 1, which means you can cover your obligations, but tighter than ideal," Mo observed. "What could you do to strengthen it?"

Greg thought for a moment. "I could build up more cash reserves. Or reduce some of the current liabilities by paying them down."

"You got it! These ratios aren't just abstract numbers; they're early warning systems," Mo explained. "When they start moving in the wrong direction, you can take action before a real problem develops."

Mo laughed. "We won't go any deeper today. But these are trail markers, Greg. They tell you if you're on solid ground or headed for trouble."

They continued riding, the trail gradually circling back toward the parking lot.

"Here's a practical exercise," Mo said. "Draft a simple Balance Sheet tonight. What you own, what you owe. Then ask yourself, if a major client cancelled tomorrow, how long could you operate? If your mower broke, could you replace it? The answers are in your Balance Sheet."

"I'll do it tonight."

"Good. And here's something to consider. A Balance Sheet tells you about financial position, but not about opportunity costs."

Greg gave Mo a questioning look.

"What you could have done with the same resources," Mo explained. "Buy a new mower or invest in marketing? Pay down debt or build cash reserves? The Balance Sheet shows results, not the decisions that led there."

The trail joined a wider gravel path for the final stretch to the parking lot.

"Your father would tell you that a clean Balance Sheet with minimal debt is always best," Mo said. "And there's wisdom in that.

But sometimes strategic debt fuels growth that wouldn't happen otherwise."

"Which is right?"

"Both. Neither. Depends on your goals, risk tolerance, and timing." Mo slowed as they approached the parking area. "That's the art part of the science."

They reached the trucks and dismounted. Greg's legs felt rubbery from the exertion, but his mind was racing with connections.

As they loaded the bikes onto Mo's rack, Greg found himself unusually quiet, his mind processing more than just the lessons of the climb.

Mo noticed. "Something on your mind, Greggo?"

Greg secured Mo's bike, buying time to organize his thoughts. "Do you ever doubt yourself? Even after all your success?"

Mo leaned against the truck, studying Greg with newfound interest. "All the time. Anyone who says they don't is either lying or lacking self-awareness."

"Even now?" Greg pressed. "After building a successful company and selling it?"

"Especially then." Mo's voice grew quieter, more reflective. "The higher you climb, the farther there is to fall. The more you build, the more you have to lose."

Greg's shoulders relaxed, relieved he wasn't alone in his feelings. "Lately I've been having these moments of... I don't know, panic? One minute I'm confident about growing the business, the next I'm wondering if I'm just fooling myself."

"The entrepreneur's pendulum," Mo said with a knowing smile. "Swinging between 'I'm going to change the world' and 'Who am I kidding?'"

"Exactly!" Greg exclaimed. "Yesterday I signed two new clients and felt invincible. This morning I woke up at 3 a.m. worried about equipment breaking down and losing everything."

Mo opened the truck door and grabbed two bottles of water, handing one to Greg. "You know what I've learned? That pendulum never stops swinging. You just learn to ride it better."

"How?" Greg asked, the single word carrying the weight of genuine uncertainty.

"By separating feelings from facts." Mo tapped Greg's backpack where his financial records were stored. "That's why all these tools matter. When doubt creeps in, you don't have to rely on feelings. You can look at actual data—cash flow projections, client retention rates, profit margins. The numbers tell you where you truly stand."

Greg took a long drink of water, considering this. "My dad never seems to doubt himself. He's always so... certain."

"*Quizás*. Or maybe he's just better at hiding it." Mo shrugged. "Either way, doubt isn't your enemy. It keeps you humble, makes you double-check your assumptions, forces you to prepare for contingencies."

"But it's exhausting sometimes."

"It is," Mo agreed. "That's why you need systems and routines to fall back on. Regular financial reviews, clear decision criteria, contingency plans. They create a foundation solid enough to stand on even when your confidence wavers."

Greg remembered the projected P&L they'd created, how it had given him clarity about pricing and costs when he'd been uncertain.

"So the doubt never goes away, but the tools help you manage it?" Greg asked.

"The tools, and something else." Mo reached into the truck again, this time pulling out his worn notebook, the landscaping business ledger he'd mentioned to Greg once. He flipped to a page near the back and handed it to Greg.

The page contained a column of numbers, dates spanning years, with dollar figures beside them. Some entries had brief notes.

"What am I looking at?" Greg asked.

"Every time I hit a significant revenue milestone," Mo explained. "First $1,000 month. First $10,000 month. First $100,000 quarter. And so on."

Greg noticed something interesting. "The time between milestones gets shorter."

"Momentum builds," Mo affirmed. "Like a bike picking up speed on a long descent. Early progress is slow, but it accelerates."

He turned the page to reveal a different list. Client names, with dates and brief descriptions of problems solved.

"And these are reminders of impact," Mo continued. "Times when our work made a real difference for clients. The city park we renovated that became a neighborhood gathering place. The elementary school where we fixed drainage issues that had plagued them for years."

"You keep track of all this?"

"It's my antidote to doubt," Mo said simply. "When that pendulum swings toward uncertainty, I remember how far I've come and why the journey matters."

Greg handed the notebook back, thinking about his own business. He hadn't been tracking milestones or impact moments, just numbers and operations. Perhaps there was another dimension to business success that went beyond financial statements.

"For what it's worth," Mo added, closing the notebook, "you're further along at this stage than I was when I started. You're asking better questions, building stronger systems, and planning more strategically."

The compliment caught Greg off guard. Mo wasn't one for empty praise.

"Thanks," he managed, feeling a flush of pride mixed with gratitude. He knew that he would have very little of it without Uncle Mo.

"Don't thank me. You did the work."

Greg found himself thinking about the emotional side of entrepreneurship, how managing your mindset was as crucial as managing your cash flow. The doubts might never disappear completely, but perhaps, like the mountain they'd just climbed, they became more manageable with experience, proper equipment, and a clear understanding of the terrain.

"The three statements—P&L, Balance Sheet, and Cash Flow—they're like different perspectives on the same landscape," Greg said, unlocking his bike rack. "P&L is looking at the trail through time. Balance Sheet is the overlook view at one moment. And Cash Flow…"

"Is feeling the terrain under your wheels," Mo finished. "Actually experiencing the bumps and flows."

As Greg loaded his bike, Mo pulled a folder from his truck.

"Here's something for you to study." He handed Greg several sheets of paper. "These are the financial statements from my landscaping business's third year. Look at how they connect and what story they tell together."

Greg flipped through the pages. "The net income on the P&L…"

43

"Matches the equity change on the Balance Sheet, minus distributions I took," Mo confirmed. "And the cash balance at the end of the Cash Flow Statement…"

"Is the same as cash on the Balance Sheet." Greg looked up, understanding dawning. "They're telling the same story from different angles."

"Now you're getting it." Mo closed his tailgate. "Next time, we'll focus on that Cash Flow Statement, the most important report for a new business owner."

Greg carefully placed the folder in his backpack with his notebook. "Thanks, Uncle Mo. This is making more sense than it ever did when Dad explained it."

"That's because you're building something real now. I think his explanations might make more sense to you now that the numbers have meaning." Mo checked his watch. "I've got a nonprofit board meeting at noon. But before I go…did you notice something about the bike you rode today?"

Greg glanced at the trail bike he'd just returned to Mo. "It handled the terrain perfectly."

"Because it was built for specifically this kind of riding." Mo tapped the frame. "Every component chosen for a specific purpose, balanced against weight, cost, and durability."

"Like a well-structured Balance Sheet."

Mo grinned. "You're catching on, kid. Finding the right balance isn't just good accounting; it's good business and good living." He opened his truck door. "One last thing. Cash might be king, but a strong Balance Sheet is what lets you sleep at night."

As Mo's truck pulled away, Greg remained standing in the parking lot, the morning's lessons settling into place. The trail they'd ridden—with its obstacles, decisions, and moments of flow—had shown him more about business fundamentals than any textbook ever could.

He opened his notebook and jotted down a final thought:

Build a business that can weather the terrain ahead, not just the terrain you can see.

THE FLOW

TWO MONTHS INTO his lawn business, Greg had settled into a routine. Instead of mornings at his regular job, evenings and weekends dedicated to building his side hustle, his business had quickly become his full-time gig. Seventeen clients now, each paying twenty-five dollars per cut. The notebook Mo had given him was filling with numbers, observations, and questions.

His phone buzzed late Thursday afternoon as he finished up Mr. Chen's yard.

"How's it going, Greggo?" Mo's voice came through the speaker.

"Just wrapped up client number seven," Greg replied, wiping sweat from his forehead. "Starting to see a rhythm to it."

"Good. Any rain days yet?"

"Not so far."

"Mmm." Mo's tone suggested he knew that luck wouldn't last. "Stop by the house tomorrow afternoon. Time to talk cash flow."

Greg arrived at Mo's place just after 4pm the next day. Unlike their previous meetings, Mo was waiting in his home office rather than the garage. The space reflected its owner. Organized yet lived-in, with bookshelves lining one wall and large windows overlooking the backyard. A desk dominated one corner, its surface covered with papers and a laptop connected to an extra monitor.

"Welcome to command central," Mo said, gesturing Greg to a chair. "Thought we'd stay indoors today."

"No bikes?" Greg asked, half-joking.

"Not today. But we'll get back to that." Mo cleared a space on his desk. "You've been running your business for a couple months now. Let's see your numbers."

Greg pulled out his notebook and flipped to the most recent entries. "Seventeen clients, $425 weekly revenue. Averaging about $75 per week for gas and other variable expenses."

Mo glanced at the notebook and tapped on the page with his finger. "Good tracking. Let me ask you something. When do you feel richest?"

"What do you mean?"

"In your business. When does your wallet feel heaviest?"

Greg thought about it. "Friday evenings, I guess. After I've collected from everyone but before I've had to pay for the next week's gas and maintenance."

"And when do you feel poorest?"

"Thursday mornings. Right before I start the rounds but after I've paid for all my supplies."

Mo smiled. "You've just described cash flow. The ebb and surge of money through your business." He turned to his laptop and opened a spreadsheet. "This is what we're talking about today, The Cash Flow Statement."

Greg leaned forward. The spreadsheet looked different from the P&L and Balance Sheet they'd discussed before.

"This is from a landscaping business I advised last year. I use it as a teaching example because it shows everything so clearly."

At the top were columns for every balance sheet account: Cash & Equivalents, Accounts Receivable, Other Current Assets, Fixed Assets, Accounts Payable, Credit Cards, and so on across the full spectrum of the balance sheet. The spreadsheet showed a horizontal layout of balance sheet accounts across the top. Assets were represented as positive numbers, liabilities and equity as negative numbers. Below these were rows showing beginning balances, ending balances, and the differences between them.

	A	B C D	E	F G H	I J	K	L M	N O	P	Q R	S
1	John's Landscaping										
2	Statement of Cash Flows										
3											
4		Cash &	Accounts		Fixed	Accum	Accounts	Credit		Balance
5		Equiv	Receivable	Inventory	Assets	Depr	Payable	Cards	R/E	Check
6										
7	Ending Balance	23,000	13,500	4,000	50,000	(22,000)	(4,000)	(1,500)	(63,000)	·
8	Beginning Balance	21,000	10,000	5,000	49,000	(20,000)	(8,000)	(2,000)	(55,000)	·
9	Change	2,000	3,500	(1,000)	1,000	(2,000)	4,000	500	(8,000)	·
10										
11	CASH FLOWS FROM OPERATING ACTIVITIES									
12	Net income (loss)	8,000							(8,000)	·
13	Adjustments to reconcile net income to net									
14	cash provided by (used in) operating activities									
15	Depreciation	2,000				(2,000)				·
16	(Increase) Decrease in Accounts Receivable	(3,500)	3,500							·
17	(Increase) Decrease in Inventory	1,000		(1,000)						·
18	Increase (Decrease) in Accounts Payable	(4,000)					4,000			·
19	NET CASH PROVIDED BY (USED IN) OPERATING ACTIVITIES	3,500	3,500	(1,000)	-	(2,000)	4,000	-	(8,000)	·
20										
21	CASH FLOWS FROM INVESTING ACTIVITIES									
22	Acquisition of Fixed Assets	(1,000)			1,000					·
23	Proceeds from Disposals of Fixed Assets	-			-					·
24	NET CASH PROVIDED BY (USED IN) INVESTING ACTIVITIES	(1,000)	-	-	1,000	-	-	-	-	·
25										
26	CASH FLOWS FROM FINANCING ACTIVITIES									
27	Repayments of Credit Cards	(500)						500		·
28	NET CASH PROVIDED BY (USED IN) FINANCING ACTIVITIES	(500)	-	-	-	-	-	500	-	·
29										
30	NET INCREASE (DECREASE) IN CASH AND EQUIV.	2,000	3,500	(1,000)	1,000	(2,000)	4,000	500	(8,000)	·
31										
32	Balance Check (Must Equal -0-)	·	·	·	·	·	·	·	·	·
33										

"Remember how we said the three financial statements articulate with each other?" Mo asked. "The Cash Flow Statement is where it all comes together. It shows how your P&L performance translates into movement on your Balance Sheet, especially cash."

"That sounds complex."

"It can be. But I've found a way to visualize it that makes sense." Mo turned the laptop toward Greg. "This isn't how they teach it in accounting textbooks, but it works for real business owners."

"Traditional Cash Flow Statements are formatted vertically," Mo explained, "like you see here." Mo pointed to the cash flow statement along the left margin of the spreadsheet. "But I use this horizontal approach to preparing it because it shows you how each

49

balance sheet account changed during the period, and whether that change provided or used cash."

"This horizontal layout shows everything at once," Mo explained. "See these three rows at the top? The first shows where each account stood at the end of the period, the second shows where they started, and the third—this 'Change' row—shows exactly how much each account increased or decreased."

Greg leaned closer, studying the screen.

"Now watch how this connects to cash flow," Mo said, pointing to a negative figure in the Cash column. "Their cash decreased during this period. The reason must be found in the changes to all other balance sheet accounts."

He traced his finger across the Change row. "Accounts Receivable increased significantly. That's a use of cash because it's money earned but not collected yet. Other Current Assets decreased. That's a source of cash. Accounts Payable increased. Another source of cash since you received goods or services without paying for them yet."

Greg looked confused. "Accounts payable is a source of cash? How is that?"

Mo smiled. "I know. Sounds a little counterintuitive, right? Accounts Payable is something you pay, so how can it be a source of cash? Well, think about it for a minute. What happens when you pay your Accounts Payable?"

"I take my cash out and I pay my vendors."

"Right. So if paying your Accounts Payable takes your cash, then *not* paying your Accounts Payable means you have more cash in your pocket, right?"

"I guess that makes sense."

"So if your Accounts Payable decreases when you use your cash to pay them, then it's logical that not paying your Accounts Payable isn't a use of cash, but a source of cash. Not paying your vendors means you have cash for something else, at least theoretically."

Greg's eyes widened with understanding. "So each change in my balance sheet accounts, up or down, either provides or uses cash?"

"That's right. And they must all balance out perfectly," Mo confirmed. "But you have to think about it, because assets and liabilities perform differently. Simplistically speaking, when an asset other than cash increases, it's a use of cash, because you had to use cash to buy the asset. But when a liability increases, it's a source of cash, because you didn't use cash to decrease it."

Greg was beginning to understand, but he still had questions. "An increase in a liability an increase in cash because you didn't decrease it. That almost sounds like a double negative," he quipped.

"I get what you're saying, and it sort of does. I know it sounds wordy, but I said it like that to force you to think it through. Your dad can even get that backwards sometimes if he doesn't stop to think about it."

"I see. So it's not always a literal movement of cash to or from a specific asset or liability. Inventory might increase when I buy supplies from a vendor, but if I bought those supplies on account, then my liability goes up by the same amount. If the amounts are the same, then there's no effect on cash."

"Right! So you're looking at the net change in each of your assets and liabilities, and the sum of all those net changes is your net change in cash."

"Ahhh," Greg sighed, as the pieces started coming together. "So cash flow is like seeing how the balance sheet changes over time. Like you said before."

"Like I said before. Once you identify all the changes in the balance sheet, then you organize those changes into categories."

"Categories? Like variable and fixed expenses?"

"Not exactly. It's more like, I don't know, sections."

Still not clear, Greg said it back to Mo, "Sections?"

"Look. The sections over here to the left organize these same changes into traditional cash flow categories—operating, investing, and financing activities—but the horizontal view makes it easier to see exactly where the cash went."

Mo pointed to Net Income at the top of the column. "This business was profitable that month, but their cash still decreased. This layout shows you exactly why. Their accounts receivable grew significantly, meaning they were waiting on customer payments, and they paid down some short-term debt. The money had to go somewhere, and this shows you precisely where."

Greg studied the screen. "So the difference between the beginning and ending balance of each account…"

"Tells you how much cash moved through that account." Mo pointed again to the accounts receivable column. "See here? When receivables go up, that's a use of cash. You've done the work but haven't been paid yet." Using his finger, he traced down the screen until he was even with the line on the Cash Flow Statement to the left that said Accounts Receivable. Then traced over to the left to make sure Greg's eyes made the connection. "When receivables go down, that's a source of cash. Clients are paying their outstanding invoices."

"I see," Greg eyes moved back up to the balance sheets across the top and found Accounts Payable. "And for AP," pointing at the number he'd found, then tracing it down, "went down as well, which is also a use of cash, because you *used cash* to pay a vendor."

"Right! So every change in a balance sheet account up here," referring to the beginning and ending balance sheets across the top of the page, "gets reflected over here," referring to the calculated Cash Flow Statement on the left. "I use formulas to compute the amount of the change, another formula to bring it down here even with the right line item on the Cash Flow, and a formula on the Cash Flow itself to reflect the change."

Looking at the formulas in the toolbar in Excel, Greg noticed something. "Why do some of the formulas have a minus sign, and some don't?"

"Good eye! That's because increases and decreases in assets and increases and decreases in liabilities have the opposite effect on cash flow. They operate in reverse."

"Ahh. Right. Like when AR increased, it was a *use* of cash and when AP increased it was a *source* of cash."

"Yes. Sources and uses, increases and decreases, that's just different ways of talking about the same thing."

Sensing that Greg still had questions, Mo continued to elaborate. "I know we haven't talked a lot about the *natural balance* of accounts, but I suspect that you might remember a little something about that from your chats with your dad."

"Oh yeah. That seemed super confusing at the time. Assets had natural debit balances and liabilities and equity had natural credit balances, right?"

Seeing Mo smile in knowing affirmation he went on. "Which makes a ton more sense to me now. They're on opposites sides of the balance sheet."

Then all at once, something dawned on Greg as he was looking at the balance sheets across the top of the spreadsheet. "Wait! I just noticed the balance sheet on your spreadsheet. I mean, I know you mentioned this, but the weight of it didn't strike me until now. That's why you show assets as positive numbers and liabilities as negative numbers. It's not that their balances are positive or negative, but you needed a way to show that their natural balances were opposite."

"I'm impressed! That's usually one of the first questions I get asked when I show somebody this, and you've already figured it out."

"I just figured it was your way of making sure that the balance sheet balance. I saw your SUM formula off to the right that showed zero for the total."

"Yeah, it's that, too." Mo seemed genuinely impressed. "Every once in a while, though, the natural balance isn't what you expect. Like with accumulated depreciation. That resides on the asset side of the balance sheet."

"Because it's a contra-asset," Greg finished his thought. "It goes against Fixed Assets, reducing its carrying value. Hmph. I guess I recall more of what Dad said than I thought!"

"Clearly! And what did your dad say about the Cash Flow Statement?"

"Not much really. He talked about it now and then, but usually in the context of how hard it was to prepare or in frustration when his accounting software couldn't just spit it out for him like it did the other statements."

"I'm sure they've gotten better," Mo responded. "But reporting cash flow has always seemed elusive, to professionals and software developers alike. Maybe I should share my spreadsheet with them?"

Greg laughed. "Maybe!"

Mo smiled. "Maybe they could figure out how to automate it. I still have to make some manual adjustments to get it just right. Like, Accumulated Depreciation goes up when I post my depreciation journal entries, but it also goes down when I dispose of an asset and remove the associated Accumulated Depreciation. Depreciation Expense affects the Operating section of the Cash Flow Statement, and asset disposal is an Investing activity."

"So how do you handle that?" Greg asked, intrigued.

"I just manually split the net change in Accumulated Depreciation between the two line items. I'm sure there's probably a way to automate that, but it was never worth it to me to take the time to figure it out since it was so easy to fix it manually."

"Makes sense. Still, manual or not, your spreadsheet makes it so clear to me. The changes in the balance sheet from the beginning of the period to the end of the period here," he drew his finger across the third row showing the computed changes, "relate directly to the cash flow increases and decreases, the various sources and uses over the same period," drawing his finger from top to bottom down the Cash Flow Statement on the left.

"You got it. Now let me show something *really* interesting," Mo said, reaching for Greg's notebook. He flipped to the back and drew a simple stick figure at the bottom of the last page. "Your Balance Sheet is like a snapshot, right? One moment frozen in time."

He turned to the previous page and drew the same figure, but with its arms raised slightly. Then he continued backward through several pages, each time drawing the figure with slightly different positions.

"Now watch this," Mo said, holding the edge of the pages with his thumb. He let them flip rapidly from back to front, and suddenly the stick figure appeared to move, raising its arms above its head.

"That, Greggo, is the Cash Flow Statement," Mo explained, tapping the notebook. "Each page is a Balance Sheet at a different moment. When you flip through them in sequence, you see movement--the story of how things changed over time. The P&L tells you why the figure is moving, but the Cash Flow Statement shows you the actual movement between static positions. It's like watching the Balance Sheet come alive through time."

Greg's eyes widened with understanding. "So the Cash Flow Statement is like the animation that connects two different Balance Sheet positions..."

"Right! It's essentially looking at the Balance Sheet over time, showing how and why each account changed between two points. It reveals which Balance Sheet changes were caused by P&L activities and which came from other sources, like buying equipment or securing loans. That's why cash flow is where the P&L meets the Balance Sheet--it connects your performance to your position, showing how one transformed into the other."

Greg held his mouth slightly open, taking it all in.

Mo noticed and smiled with appreciation and even affection. "You just had an *a-ha* moment, didn't you?"

Greg closed his mouth and managed to grunt, "Mmmhmm," still marveling at the insight.

"Now, let me make this concrete with your lawn business," Mo said, pulling a blank piece of paper from the desk drawer. "Say you mow Mrs. Abernathy's lawn for twenty-five dollars, but she won't pay you until next week. What happens on your financial statements?"

Greg thought for a moment. "On my P&L, I'd record twenty-five dollars in revenue."

"Right. And on your Balance Sheet?"

"My accounts receivable would increase by twenty-five dollars."

"Perfect. But did any actual cash change hands yet?"

"No," Greg realized. "I did the work but haven't received any cash."

"*Mucho trabajo y poco dinero,*" Mo mumbled to himself. *Lots of work and little money.* Then he leaned over and drew a simple diagram showing the transaction. "This is where the Cash Flow Statement bridges the understanding gap. It would show that while you earned revenue on the P&L. It's imbedded in your net income number at the top of the cash flow statement. That revenue didn't generate cash yet. It's sitting in accounts receivable... here, where AR is up by twenty-five dollars. Then, on next week's cash flow, when Mrs. Abernathy pays you, no new revenue appears on the P&L, but on the Balance Sheet, cash goes up twenty-five dollars and accounts receivable goes down twenty-five dollars."

"And the Cash Flow Statement would show the cash actually arriving," Greg said, the concept clicking into place.

"Correct. Now imagine this happening with dozens of clients, some equipment purchases, loan payments, and various expenses, all on different timelines. The Cash Flow Statement tracks all that movement, showing you exactly when money flows in and out, regardless of when it was earned or incurred."

Greg's facial expression showed a strange tension between understanding and confusion. "That makes sense! But tell me again, how does this tie back to the P&L?"

"Your net income is where the Cash Flow Statement starts." Mo scrolled up to show the top section. "Then you adjust for anything that affected net income but not cash, like depreciation. You also adjust for anything that affected cash but not income, like buying equipment or paying down loans. These show up in the investing and financing sections of the statement."

Greg seemed to be getting it, but Mo could tell he still had questions spinning around in his head.

"Let me give you a more specific example from your lawn business," Mo continued. "Last month you recorded $2,500 in revenue on your P&L, but you only collected $2,100 in cash because some clients paid late. You also bought that new edger for $300, which doesn't show on your P&L except as small monthly depreciation. And you made that $150 payment on your mower loan, but only $25 of that was interest expense on your P&L; the rest was principal reduction."

Greg nodded slowly. "So my P&L showed a profit of just over $1,400, but my actual cash increased by... let's see... $2,100 minus operating expenses, minus $300 for the edger, minus $150 for the loan payment...just under $600?"

"You're almost there. Don't forget about your depreciation expense," Mo reminded him. "That's included in your operating expenses, right?"

"Of course!" Greg almost looked excited, an emotion he'd never thought he'd associate with accounting. "And that's a non-cash expense, so I have to add that back!" Greg was smiling, like someone who found $10 in his pocket while doing laundry.

"Yep," Mo said. "Without adding that back, what you originally calculated didn't match the actual change in your cash balance. That's how I knew something was missing."

"I see. The P&L showed the depreciation, but I forgot about that when I was trying to figure it out in my head."

"Exactly. And that's why you need all three statements to get the complete picture of your financial health. The numbers tell different parts of the same story."

As intricate as it sounded, the visual layout made the concept clearer than Greg expected.

"The beauty of this approach," Mo continued, "is that it forces the Cash Flow Statement to balance with your other statements. When you drop your balance sheet balances into the worksheet, it serves as a cross-check for both your Balance Sheet and P&L. Net Income is a component of Equity, specifically, Retained Earnings. The change in Equity usually equals your Net Income."

"I see," Greg acknowledged. "So the $1,415 of Net Income from my P&L equals my change in Retained Earnings shown on my Balance Sheet," pointing to the top right of the worksheet.

"Right. Your Cash Flow Statement starts where your P&L ends—with Net Income—and ends with the net change in cash. The net change in cash shown here," Mo said, pointing first to the Net Income line at the top left, then dragging his finger down to the result shown at the bottom of the worksheet, "must equal the difference between your beginning and ending cash balance at the top of your Balance Sheet."

"It's almost like a check-figure," Greg added, almost to himself.

	A	B	C	D	E	F	G	H	I	J	K	L	M	N	O	P	Q
1	Greg's Lawns																
2	Statement of Cash Flows																
3																	
4					Cash &		Accounts		Fixed		Accum	Accounts		Loan			Balance
5					Equiv		Receivable		Assets		Depr	Payable		Payable		R/E	Check
6																	
7	Ending Balance				3,800		400		2,300		(10)	-		(1,875)		(4,415)	•
8	Beginning Balance				3,000		-		2,000		-	-		(2,000)		(3,000)	•
9	Change				800		400		300		(10)	-		125		(1,415)	•
10																	
11	CASH FLOWS FROM OPERATING ACTIVITIES																
12	Net Income (loss)				1,415											(1,415)	•
13	Adjustments to reconcile net income to net																
14	cash provided by (used in) operating activities																
15	Depreciation				10						(10)						•
16	(Increase) Decrease in Accounts Receivable				(400)		400										•
17	(Increase) Decrease in Inventory				-												•
18	Increase (Decrease) in Accounts Payable				-												•
19	NET CASH PROVIDED BY (USED IN) OPERATING ACTIVITIES				1,025		400		-		(10)	-		-		(1,415)	•
20																	
21	CASH FLOWS FROM INVESTING ACTIVITIES																
22	Acquisition of Fixed Assets				(300)				300								•
23	Proceeds from Disposals of Fixed Assets				-				-								
24	NET CASH PROVIDED BY (USED IN) INVESTING ACTIVITIES				(300)		-		300		-	-		-		-	•
25																	
26	CASH FLOWS FROM FINANCING ACTIVITIES																
27	Repayments of Credit Cards				(125)									125			•
28	NET CASH PROVIDED BY (USED IN) FINANCING ACTIVITIES				(125)		-		-		-	-		125		-	•
29																	
30	NET INCREASE (DECREASE) IN CASH AND EQUIV.				800		400		300		(10)	-		125		(1,415)	•
31																	
32	Balance Check (Must Equal -0-)				•		•		•		•	•		•		•	•
33																	

"It is exactly that. And see these dashes down the right-hand side and at the bottom? That's how the spreadsheet formats as zeroes. These are all check-figures, to make sure you haven't missed anything."

"This makes cash flow visual in a way I've never seen before," Greg said.

"That's the point. Traditional cash flow statements hide the connections. This approach reveals them," Mo said. "Every dollar that doesn't stay in your cash account moves somewhere else on your balance sheet. When you can see those movements clearly, you can manage them strategically."

"They each tell a story," Greg said, remembering their previous conversation.

"Right. When all three statements tell the same story from different angles, you know your numbers are right." Mo closed the laptop. "But enough theory. Let's make this real. Grab your notebook. We're heading out."

Mo led Greg to his truck rather than the garage. "We're going to El Diablo Trail. I already loaded our gear."

Greg raised his eyebrows. El Diablo was notorious among local mountain bikers. Steep ascents, technical descents, and a section aptly named "The Decision Maker" where riders had to choose between three equally challenging routes.

"I'm not sure I'm ready for El Diablo."

"Nobody ever is." Mo started the engine. "That's what makes it perfect for today's lesson."

Twenty minutes later, they unloaded their bikes at the trailhead. Mo had brought his high-end trail bike for Greg again. The late afternoon sun cast long shadows across the parking area as they geared up.

"Cash flow is about timing and momentum," Mo said, checking his tire pressure. "Today you'll feel that in your legs and your decisions."

They set off, the trail immediately pitching upward. Unlike their previous rides, Mo set a punishing pace from the start.

"Keep up!" he called back. "We need momentum for what's coming!"

Greg pushed hard, legs burning as they climbed. Just as he thought he couldn't maintain the pace, the trail leveled briefly before dropping into a rocky section.

"Don't brake!" Mo shouted ahead. "Let your momentum carry you!"

Greg fought his instinct to slow down, instead letting the bike roll through the rock garden. To his surprise, the speed made the section easier. His wheels rolled over obstacles rather than getting caught between them.

They emerged onto a flat section, both breathing hard.

"That," Mo said between breaths, "is lesson one. Sometimes you need speed to survive obstacles."

"What's that got to do with cash flow?"

"Growth creates momentum. Sometimes rapid expansion is exactly what you need to get you through rough patches." Mo took a drink from his water bottle. "But not always."

They continued riding, the trail alternating between technical sections and smooth flow. After about two miles, they reached a section where the path narrowed and wound through deep, soft sand.

"Watch me," Mo called, slowing dramatically as he entered the sand. He feathered his brakes and kept his upper body loose, allowing the front wheel to wander slightly while maintaining forward progress.

Greg tried to follow the same line but came in too fast. His front wheel dug in, stopping abruptly and sending him over the handlebars, faceplanting into the sand.

"You good?" Mo circled back.

Greg stood, brushing sand from his clothes. "Yeah. What happened?"

"Too much speed in the wrong conditions." Mo helped him right his bike. "In sand, slower is often better. Controlled movement beats forceful pushing."

Greg remounted, this time approaching the sand with deliberate patience. The bike wobbled but remained upright as he made it through.

"Cash flow has these same dynamics," Mo explained when they regrouped. "Sometimes you need to push hard and grow quickly. Other times, slowing down and conserving resources is the smarter move."

They rode further, eventually stopping at a ridge overlooking the valley. The sun had begun its descent, painting the landscape in warm hues.

"Let me tell you about a client I once advised," Mo said as they caught their breath. "Landscaping company, not unlike what I built. He was growing fast, winning new contracts every month. Revenue climbing steadily."

"Sounds successful."

"On paper, sure. P&L looked great. Increasing revenue. Healthy profit margins. Balance Sheet showed growing assets. But his Cash Flow Statement told a different story."

"What was happening?"

"Four things, all colliding." Mo held up fingers as he counted. "Some he could control, some he couldn't. First, rain days. Lots of them. When it rains, no work happens, but payroll continues."

"You can't control the weather," Greg contributed.

"No, sure can't. And sometimes, like riding fast in the rain, it stings." Mo went on. "Second, he decided to upgrade his entire truck fleet at once. Seven new vehicles, all financed."

"And buying new trucks was a bad idea?" Greg asked, thinking about a big purchase of his own that he was considering but hadn't yet mentioned to anyone.

"Good long-term decision, just terrible timing. Next, several large projects had large unpaid invoices, at least one of which never paid. And last, and most dangerous, his personal distributions exceeded his actual profits."

Greg frowned. "How is that possible? If the business was profitable…"

"Growth masked the problem. As the business expanded, more cash was tied up in receivables, equipment, and inventory, but payables and other short-term debt surged as well. His bank account looked healthy because of the constant inflow from new clients and the various fluctuations in his balance sheet, but after the dust settled, it was clear that he was actually pulling out more than the business was generating."

"Like a Ponzi scheme," Greg observed.

"Similar, except he was fooling himself, not others." Mo took another drink from his water bottle. "His year-over-year revenue still showed impressive growth. But when that growth rate just slightly declined. Not even an actual revenue drop, just slower growth. Suddenly there was no cash."

"What happened to him?"

"Nearly lost everything. Had to downsize, return some equipment, and stop taking distributions for almost a year." Mo shook his head. "All because he didn't understand cash flow."

They remounted their bikes and continued on the trail, which now followed the ridgeline before beginning a long descent.

"The Cash Flow Statement would have warned him," Mo said as they rode. "It's like riding a familiar trail in unfamiliar conditions. Same path, different experience."

They rounded a bend and Mo stopped suddenly. They had arrived at the trail intersection that Greg had feared since they left the parking lot. Ahead, the trail split into three distinct paths. They all dropped steeply down the ridge but taking different approaches.

"Welcome to The Decision Maker," Mo announced. "Three routes to the same destination. Choose wrong, and you'll either crash or have to dismount."

Greg studied the options. The left path had a sheer drop with a wooden ramp at the end. The middle was strewn with basketball-sized boulders. The right path followed a series of switchbacks, zigzagging down the slope, but then crossed a narrow wooden bridge that looked barely wider than their tires.

"Which one would you take?" Mo asked.

Greg considered. "The right seems safest."

"Based on what?"

"Less steep, no big drop or rocks."

"But that skinny bridge requires perfect balance and control," Mo pointed out. "The middle route looks challenging but allows multiple lines. The left is the most intimidating initially but actually has the cleanest exit once you commit to the drop."

Greg realized Mo was making a point beyond mountain biking. "So how do I decide?"

"Depends on your skills, your equipment, and your risk tolerance." Mo dismounted and walked to the edge. "In business, the Cash Flow Statement helps you make these kinds of decisions. It shows you not just your position, but your momentum and options."

Mo pointed down each path. "Let's say the left route is rapid expansion, taking on big contracts that require initial investment but promise significant returns. The middle is steady growth, challenging but navigable with the right approach. The right path is consolidation, slower, more controlled, but with critical moments where precision matters."

"And the best choice?"

"Depends on your cash position and projected flow." Mo remounted his bike. "Watch me take the middle, then you decide your own path."

Mo dropped in, picking a careful line through the boulders, his body loose yet controlled. He made it look easy, though Greg could see the technical skill required in each movement.

At the bottom, Mo called up: "*No problemo*," Mo quipped cheekily. "Your turn! Cash flow is about choices made in real-time with the resources you have!"

Greg studied the three options again. The left drop looked terrifying but clean, a single moment of commitment. The middle path Mo had taken required constant adjustments. The right path needed precision but less raw courage.

He chose the right path, carefully navigating the switchbacks. When he reached the narrow bridge, he focused entirely on the exit point rather than the precarious boards beneath his tires. A moment of weightlessness, then he was across and rolling down to join Mo.

"Interesting choice," Mo remarked. "Conservative entry, but that bridge crossing took serious focus. Just like managing cash through a tight spot."

They continued down the trail, eventually looping back toward the parking area as twilight settled around them.

"So how do I create a Cash Flow Statement for my business?" Greg asked as they rode.

"Start simple. Track weekly cash receipts and payments. Note timing differences between when you perform work and when you get paid." Mo navigated around a fallen branch. "As you grow, you can build something more sophisticated like the spreadsheet I showed you."

"And how does it help me make decisions?"

"When you learn to forecast it, it will answer critical questions." Mo slowed to emphasize his points. "How much cash will you have next month? If you buy that better mower, how long until the investment pays off? If a client delays payment, can you still cover your expenses? If you want to add three new clients, do you have the cash to handle the upfront costs?"

They reached a final climb before the descent to the parking lot. Mo stopped at the crest.

"Cash flow problems kill businesses that otherwise look healthy on paper." Mo's tone was serious. "Your father would focus on minimizing taxes and maintaining a clean Balance Sheet. That's important, but in a growing business, understanding cash flow is even more critical."

"It's about timing, not just totals," Greg said, beginning to see the larger picture.

"Yep. And momentum. Knowing when to push and when to conserve." Mo pointed down the final descent. "Like this last section. It's fast and flowing but has a surprise around that blind corner. Too much speed, and you'll miss the sharp turn at the bottom."

They took the descent at a measured pace, Greg following Mo's line. Sure enough, a sharp left turn appeared suddenly at the bottom, requiring quick braking to avoid running straight into the woods.

Back at the truck, as they loaded their bikes in near-darkness, Mo continued his explanation.

"The cash flow spreadsheet I showed you makes the concept visual. Assets increase? Usually a cash outflow. Liabilities increase? Usually a cash inflow. The net change across all balance sheet accounts must equal the change in your cash position."

They stood behind the truck as Mo secured the bikes. Greg shifted his weight as the idea took hold. "And this connects to the P&L through net income."

"Right. Net income is your starting point, then you adjust for non-cash items and timing differences." Mo secured the bikes. "Take depreciation. That's when your mower loses value over time. It shows up as an expense on your P&L, reducing net income, but it doesn't actually take cash out of your pocket that month. Growing receivables increases revenue but doesn't provide cash yet."

Mo paused, then added with a wry smile, "And dragging your feet on paying some of your bills preserves cash temporarily, but eventually, you'll have to pay the piper. Hopefully, you will have collected payments from your customers by then!"

In the truck on the way back, Mo handed Greg a printed spreadsheet template. "Here's a simplified version of my cash flow tool. Start tracking your business this way, and you'll see patterns emerge that aren't visible in your P&L or Balance Sheet alone."

Greg studied the template in the dim cabin light. "I think I get it. Cash flow is where the P&L meets the Balance Sheet. It translates profit into actual money movement."

"Couldn't have said it better myself." Mo smiled briefly. "It's the vital link that connects performance to position. You can be profitable but cash poor, or cash rich despite temporary losses."

Back at Mo's house, they sat at the kitchen table with cups of coffee. Mo sketched on a paper napkin.

"Think of it this way," he said, drawing three interconnected circles. "P&L shows what you earned. Balance Sheet shows what you have. Cash Flow Statement shows what moved. Together, they tell the complete story."

"So what's next for my business?" Greg asked. "Based on what we've covered so far."

Mo leaned back, considering. "Start projecting, not just tracking. Forecast your cash position three months out. Include known expenses, expected revenue, and potential issues like weather delays or equipment failures."

"Basically, anticipate the trail ahead."

"You got it. And keep some reserves for the unexpected obstacles." Mo tapped the table for emphasis. "Never forget... growth consumes cash. The faster you grow, the more working capital you need."

"Like needing more momentum for bigger obstacles."

"Now you're thinking like a business owner." Mo smiled. "There's one more thing about cash flow I want you to understand. It's not just about survival. It's about opportunity."

"How so?"

"Strong cash flow gives you options. When others are desperate, you can negotiate better terms with suppliers. When equipment goes on sale, you can buy at a discount. When competitors falter, you can acquire their clients." Mo's eyes held a gleam of hard-earned wisdom. "Cash is oxygen for a business. The flow sometimes matters even more than the amount."

Greg made a note in his book. "So for next time?"

"Complete that cash flow projection. And start thinking about growth. How fast is too fast? How slow is too slow? It's different for every business, but there's an optimal pace based on your cash position and market opportunity."

As Greg drove home that night, the lessons from El Diablo Trail echoed in his mind. The moments of needed speed, the sections requiring patience, the critical choice points, all of them paralleled the cash decisions he would face as his business grew.

He thought about the different paths at The Decision Maker and realized that business, like mountain biking, wasn't about finding the universally "right" path. It was about choosing the path that matched your resources, skills, and goals at that particular moment.

His father had always presented business finance as a set of rigid rules to follow. Mo was showing him that it was more like a dynamic sport. Principles to understand, skills to develop, and judgment to apply in ever-changing conditions.

The Cash Flow Statement wasn't just another accounting report. It was the pulse of his business, revealing its rhythm, strength, and capacity for what lay ahead.

RIGHT GEAR, RIGHT TIME

G REG'S LAWN BUSINESS had hit its stride. Twelve clients now, a mix of weekly and bi-weekly arrangements. The notebook Mo had given him was filling with numbers that told a story of modest but consistent growth. Most satisfying was the cash flow projection he'd completed. Three months mapped out with expected revenue, expenses, and reserves.

It was Sunday afternoon when Mo called.

"How's it going, Greggo? Staying dry?"

Greg glanced out his window at the rain that had been falling steadily since dawn the day before. "First rain day yesterday. Lost four cuts."

"But you were prepared, right?"

"Had it in the projection. Still hurts though." Greg had spent the morning catching up on invoicing instead of mowing.

"Good. Pain means you're learning." Mo's voice held that familiar mix of approval and challenge. "Listen, I want to talk about timing. Meet me at Lakeview Park tomorrow at 6 p.m. There's a cycling event you should see."

"What kind of event?"

"Criterium race. Tight course, lots of corners, high speed. Perfect illustration for our next lesson."

The following evening was clear and cool after the rain. Greg arrived at the park to find the normally quiet roads transformed into a race circuit. Barriers lined a one-mile loop, spectators gathering at key points. Cyclists in team colors warmed up, their expensive bikes gleaming in the early evening sun.

Mo stood near the start/finish line, two folding chairs and a cooler beside him.

"Ever watched a criterium before?" Mo asked as Greg approached.

Greg shook his head. "Just the Tour de France on TV."

"Much different animal." Mo handed Greg a race program. "Shorter, more intense, more tactical. They'll do thirty laps on this course. Tight corners, high speed, constant positioning battles."

They set up their chairs at a corner that offered a view of both the approaching straightaway and the exit. Mo pulled two sodas from the cooler.

"So what's this got to do with cash flow timing?" Greg asked.

"Everything. Watch the first few laps, and you'll start to see it."

The riders lined up, a mass of color and tense anticipation. At the starter's gun, they surged forward, the pack immediately stretching into a long line as they accelerated.

As they approached the corner where Greg and Mo sat, the leaders slowed slightly, choosing their lines carefully, while riders at the back bunched up, forced to brake harder.

"See that?" Mo pointed as the pack snaked through. "The leaders control their speed, the followers react. Same corner, different experience depending on position."

By the third lap, the pattern became clearer. The pack had settled into a rhythm, but Greg noticed certain riders consistently taking different approaches to the corner.

"Some brake early, some late," Greg observed.

"That's right." Mo leaned forward. "It's all about timing. Brake too early, you lose momentum. Brake too late, you might crash. The masters know exactly when to slow down and when to power up again."

The race continued, intensity building. On lap ten, a group of three riders broke away from the pack, working together to extend their lead.

"Watch those three," Mo said. "See how they're taking turns at the front? Each one leads for a while, then drops back to recover while drafting behind the others. It's called 'taking a pull.'"

Greg agreed. "So they're sharing the work."

"Classic cash flow strategy. Sometimes you push hard, sometimes you conserve. The key is coordination and timing."

As the race progressed, the breakaway group maintained their advantage. Behind them, the main pack organized a chase, with teams taking coordinated pulls at the front to increase the pace.

"Notice the different strategies playing out," Mo said. "The leaders are gambling that their early effort will pay off. The chase group is being more conservative, counting on the leaders to tire out."

On lap twenty-two, a rider in the chase group attacked, bridging the gap to the leaders with a tremendous solo effort. The crowd cheered as he made the junction.

"Bold move," Greg said.

"Very. But watch what happens next."

The rider who had bridged the gap sat at the back of the breakaway group, unable to take his turn at the front. After two laps, he dropped off, drifting back to the chase pack.

"He spent everything getting there," Mo explained. "No reserves left."

Greg's fists clenched in frustration. "That's painful to watch. All that effort wasted." He could almost feel the rider's disappointment, the burning legs and lungs with nothing to show for it.

"He spent everything getting there," Mo explained. "No reserves left. Classic cash flow mistake. Expending all your resources on a single push with nothing left for what comes after."

As the race entered its final laps, the dynamics shifted again. One rider from the breakaway group began skipping turns at the front, conserving energy. The others noticed and the cooperation fractured.

"Now it's every rider for themselves," Mo said. "They've worked together to create an opportunity, but with the finish approaching, they're thinking about individual success."

In the final lap, the conserving rider attacked, opening a gap that the others couldn't close. He crossed the finish line alone, arms raised in victory.

After the awards ceremony, Mo led Greg to the registration area where riders were gathering their belongings. He approached the winner, a lean man who looked to be in his thirties but with the weathered look of a veteran racer.

"Great race, Marcus," Mo said, extending his hand.

"Mo! Didn't know you were here." The rider grinned, shaking Mo's hand. "Still riding yourself?"

"Recreational only these days. This is my nephew, Greg."

Marcus smiled at Greg. "Nice to meet you."

"That was impressive," Greg said. "Especially how you saved energy at the end."

Marcus laughed. "Had to. I'm forty-one competing against guys in their twenties. Can't match their raw power anymore, so I have to be smarter about energy management."

"Mind if Greg asks you about that?" Mo asked. "He's learning about resource allocation."

"Sure." Marcus took a long drink from his water bottle. "What do you want to know?"

Greg thought for a moment. "How did you know when to conserve and when to push?"

"Experience, mostly. I've blown up enough times to learn my limits." Marcus began packing his gear. "But I also track everything... power output, heart rate, nutrition timing. Data tells you when you're approaching redline."

"And today's race?"

"I knew the course had eight corners per lap. Each corner requires braking, then reacceleration; that's where most energy is spent. So I calculated how many matches I could burn before running out." Marcus zipped his bag. "I guess you could say that I set a budget," winking slyly at Mo, "and stuck to it, no matter how tempting it was to chase every move."

Mo smiled appreciatively. "You see, Greg? Timing isn't just about the clock; it's about resources and limitations."

They thanked Marcus and walked back toward the parking area. The sunset painted the sky in deep oranges and purples as race staff dismantled the course barriers.

As they approached their cars, Greg's curiosity about Mo's deep knowledge of racing tactics got the better of him.

"You seem to know a lot about competitive cycling," Greg observed. "Did you race yourself?"

75

Mo's expression shifted subtly, a ghost of a smile that suggested memories both proud and bittersweet.

"In another life," he said after a moment. "Back in Cuba, before our family came to the States. I was good. Not great, but good enough to train with some who became great."

Greg hadn't heard Mo talk much about Cuba before. "What was that like?"

Mo leaned against his truck, gazing across the darkening park where race staff were dismantling the last of the barriers.

"We trained in conditions most American cyclists couldn't imagine," he said. "Borrowed equipment, roads full of potholes, no fancy nutrition. Just rice, beans, and determination." His voice carried a warmth that transcended the limitations he described. "But there was a purity to it. We rode for the love of riding and the dream of something more."

"What happened?" Greg asked.

"Life happened." Mo shrugged, but not dismissively. "Our family left Cuba when I was seventeen. Racing became, well, complicated. I stayed connected to the sport in different ways."

"As a bike shop owner," Greg said, remembering Mo's earlier stories.

"Among other things." Mo straightened up. "But the lessons stayed with me. How to pace yourself through different terrain, when to conserve and when to attack, how to read conditions and adjust strategy." He tapped Greg's notebook. "The same principles that build a successful business."

Greg sensed there was more to the story. Something in Mo's tone suggested deeper connections to the sport than he was sharing. But he also recognized his uncle's signal that the conversation was shifting back to business.

"The point is," Mo continued, "timing isn't just about the clock; it's about reading conditions and making moves at the right moment. In cycling or business, the principle is the same."

As they parted ways, Greg found himself wondering about the chapters of Mo's life that remained unspoken, the journey from young Cuban cyclist to successful American entrepreneur. Perhaps someday Mo would share more of that story. For now, the lessons were what mattered.

"So that's cash flow timing? Knowing when to push and when to conserve?" Greg asked.

"That's part of it. But there's more." Mo leaned against his truck. "Let's take what we saw today and apply it to your business."

Mo pulled a notebook from his pocket. "In a typical month for your lawn service, when do most expenses hit?"

Greg thought about it. "Beginning of the month, mostly. Gas, maintenance, insurance payments."

"And when does most revenue come in?"

"Throughout the month, but heaviest at the end when I invoice the bi-weekly clients."

Mo sketched a quick graph, with time on the horizontal axis and cash on the vertical. The line dipped below zero at the start, gradually climbed, then rose sharply at the end.

"This is your monthly cash cycle," Mo said. "The dip at the beginning is your danger zone, when outlays exceed inflows. The peak at the end is your opportunity zone, when you have surplus to allocate."

Greg studied the drawing. "That matches what I feel, tight at the start, flush at the end."

"Most businesses have some version of this cycle. The question is, what do you do about it?" Mo tapped the paper. "Let me tell you about three approaches I've seen."

He drew three more lines on the graph, each following a different pattern.

"First approach: the conservative. They maintain high cash reserves to eliminate the dip entirely." Mo pointed to a line that never dropped below zero. "Safe, but potentially limits growth because capital sits idle."

"Like a rider who never attacks."

"Right, like a rider who never attacks. Second approach: the aggressive. They operate with minimal reserves, investing everything into growth." He indicated a line with deep dips and high peaks. "Maximum opportunity but high risk. One unexpected problem can wipe them out."

"Like the rider who bridged to the breakaway but couldn't maintain it."

"You're getting it. And third approach: the strategic. They maintain enough reserves to cover the predictable dips but deploy capital aggressively when opportunity appears." The third line showed moderate dips and strategic peaks. "Like our race winner; he knew when to conserve and when to attack."

Greg cocked his head slightly, almost imperceptibly. "So which is right for my business?"

"Depends on your goals, risk tolerance, and the nature of your business cycle." Mo folded the paper and handed it to Greg. "But here's what I want you to understand about timing: it's about synchronization, not just speed. *¿Comprende?*"

"Sort of?"

"In business, you need to synchronize three time frames: operational cycle, customer payment cycle, and supplier payment cycle." Mo counted them off on his fingers. "When they're aligned, cash flows smoothly. When they're misaligned, even profitable businesses struggle."

Greg took out his notebook. "How do I align them?"

"First, map them." Mo watched as Greg opened to a fresh page. "Your operational cycle is how long it takes to deliver your service. For lawn care, that's pretty quick, maybe a few hours per client."

"Right."

"Your customer payment cycle is how long between service and payment, currently same-day for some, up to two weeks for your invoiced clients."

Greg jotted a quick note in his book.

"And your supplier payment cycle is how long between when you incur costs and when you have to pay for them. Gas is immediate, but maybe your equipment store gives thirty-day terms on parts."

"I see the gaps."

"Those gaps are where cash flow pressure happens." Mo drew another diagram. "Ideally, you want customer payments to come in before supplier payments go out. When that's reversed, you're financing your customers."

Greg thought about this. "So I should try to get all customers to pay upfront?"

"That's one strategy. Or extend terms with suppliers. Or build sufficient reserves to bridge the gaps." Mo shrugged. "Different strategies for different situations."

They walked toward the park exit, streetlights flickering on as dusk deepened.

"Let me give you a concrete example from my landscaping business," Mo said. "We had commercial contracts that paid net-60. Meaning we did the work, then waited two months for payment. Meanwhile, we had weekly payroll, immediate fuel costs, and 30-day terms with our equipment suppliers."

"Major timing gap."

"Major. We were profitable on paper but constantly cash-stressed." Mo stopped at a park bench and sat down. "So I implemented three timing strategies."

Greg sat beside him, notebook ready.

Mo held up his index finger. "First, we negotiated. Got some clients to pay half upfront, half on completion. Got some suppliers to extend from thirty to forty-five days."

"Second, we staggered." A second finger joined the first. "Instead of buying all equipment at once, we created a rolling replacement schedule. Instead of hiring all at once, we added staff gradually."

A third finger completed the set. "Third, we synchronized. We aligned billing cycles with payroll cycles and supplier payment dates. Bills went out every Friday, not end-of-month. Supplier payments were scheduled for days after major client payments typically arrived."

"Did it work?"

"Transformed the business. Same revenue, same profitability, but cash flow smoothed out dramatically." Mo stood. "The point is, timing isn't just about having enough money. It's about having it when you need it."

They reached their vehicles, and Mo leaned against his truck.

"For next week, I want you to map your business cycles. Where are the gaps? Where are the pinch points? Then come up with three timing strategies you could implement."

Greg made a note. "I've been thinking about adding fertilizer service. Would that help or hurt my cash flow?"

"Depends on how you structure it." Mo looked thoughtful. "If clients pay for the full service upfront but you buy fertilizer in bulk at the start of the season, that's positive for cash flow. If you buy fertilizer for each job and invoice after, that's negative."

"So the same business decision can help or hurt cash flow depending on timing?"

"Now you're really getting it." Mo smiled. "That's why smart business owners consider three things for every decision: Will it be profitable? Is it operationally feasible? And what's the cash flow impact?"

As Greg drove home, the lessons from the criterium race replayed in his mind. The riders choosing when to attack and when to recover. The different strategies playing out simultaneously. The winner who understood his limitations and managed his resources accordingly.

His business might not move at twenty-five miles per hour around tight corners, but the principles were the same. Knowing when to push, when to conserve, and how to synchronize the moving parts.

That night, Greg spread his financial records across his kitchen table. For the first time, he looked at them not just as snapshots of revenue and expenses, but as a dynamic system with cycles, rhythms, and critical timing points.

He began to map his business cycles as Mo had suggested, noticing patterns he'd never seen before. The Monday rush of residential clients. The end-of-month concentration of invoicing tasks. The mid-month insurance and phone bills.

With each pattern he identified, Greg felt a growing sense of control. These weren't random events happening to him. They were predictable cycles he could prepare for and manage.

His father appeared in the doorway, coffee mug in hand, drawn by the unusual sight of Greg working with numbers on a Saturday night.

"At it again?" his father asked, moving closer to examine the organized chaos of receipts and handwritten notes. "What is all this?"

"Cash flow mapping," Greg said, not looking up. "Mo showed me how to track the timing of money coming in and going out."

His father studied the makeshift chart Greg had created, his eyebrows rising slightly. "You're tracking payment cycles against expense timing?"

"Yeah. See this pattern here?" Greg pointed to his notes. "Most of my clients pay at the beginning of the month, but my equipment maintenance costs hit mid-month. If I don't plan for that gap…"

"You run short when you shouldn't," his father finished, a note of surprise creeping into his voice.

His father lingered a moment longer, studying the systematic approach Greg had laid out. "This is… not bad. Not bad at all," he said quietly, then walked back toward his room.

Mo's earlier words echoed in Greg's mind: "Timing isn't just about having enough money, it's about having it when you need it."

Greg added a note to his growing list of business insights:

The right resource at the wrong time is still the wrong resource.

Just like shifting gears on a bicycle, success wasn't just about having the right equipment, it was about engaging it at precisely the right moment.

THE LONG CLIMB

THREE MONTHS HAD passed since Greg launched his lawn business. Twenty clients now, a mix of residential and small commercial properties. The cash flow projections Mo had taught him to create were proving accurate, and he'd implemented several timing strategies that smoothed out the financial cycles.

Most importantly, he'd begun to see patterns in the numbers that told a story about his business's health and potential. The P&L showed consistent profitability. The Balance Sheet reflected growing equity. The Cash Flow Statement confirmed he had the resources to weather unexpected challenges.

But now Greg faced a different kind of question: What next?

His phone buzzed. Mo's text read: *Meet me at Mountain View Road. 5 a.m. tomorrow. Leave your bike, but bring water, and energy bars. Dress in layers.*

Five in the morning? Mountain View Road led to the tallest peak in the county, a grueling eight-mile climb that gained nearly 3,000 feet of elevation. Greg texted back: *Sounds serious. What's the lesson?*

Mo's reply was cryptic: Growth and scalability. *Dress warm, the descent will be chilly.*

The next morning arrived with that peculiar stillness that precedes dawn. Greg pulled into the small parking area at the base of Mountain View Road to find Mo already there, two bikes mounted on his rack, neither one Greg's old Schwinn.

"Morning, Greggo." Mo handed him a steaming travel mug. "*Cortadito*. A double. You'll need it."

"Thanks." Greg took a grateful sip. "Five o'clock in the morning is cruel, even for you."

"Best time to start a long climb. Cool air, no traffic, and we'll catch the sunrise from the top." Mo began unloading the bikes. "Today you're riding this."

Mo set it between them. With a slight nod, he leaned it towards Greg, inviting him to take responsibility for balancing it. Resting his left hand on the seat, Greg gently ran his right hand along the top tube of a sleek Italian road bike with a carbon fiber frame, distinctive celeste paint, and *Campagnolo Record* components.

"Whoa. This looks expensive."

"It is." Mo handed him a helmet. "But it's also appropriate for what we're doing. Today's lesson isn't about making do, it's about understanding what it takes to scale."

They wheeled their bikes to the road entrance. The mountain loomed above them, its upper reaches still hidden in pre-dawn darkness. A sign indicated "Mountain View Summit: 8 miles."

"Before we start," Mo said, "tell me how your business is doing."

"Good, I think. Twenty clients, stable schedule, consistent profit margin."

"And what's your next move?"

Greg hesitated. "I've been thinking about hiring help. Maybe adding services."

"Why?"

"To grow."

Mo studied him in the dim light. "And why do you want to grow?"

The question caught Greg off guard. "Isn't that the point? To build something bigger?"

"Is it?" Mo clipped into his pedals. "Let's climb. We'll talk on the way up."

They set off, settling into a steady rhythm as the road immediately pitched upward. The gradient was manageable at first, allowing them to ride side by side on the empty pre-dawn road.

"Growth for growth's sake is a trap," Mo said after a few minutes. "Especially for small businesses. I've seen many entrepreneurs destroy profitable operations by scaling without purpose."

Greg shifted to an easier gear as the incline increased slightly. "So you're saying I shouldn't try to grow?"

"I'm saying you should know why you're growing and what kind of growth serves your goals." Mo maintained a measured cadence. "There are different types of growth, each with different cash flow implications."

The road curved around a bend, revealing a series of switchbacks ahead.

"Look up there," Mo said, nodding toward the mountain. "We can't see the summit yet, just the path immediately ahead. Business growth is similar. You have an ultimate destination, but you need to focus on the section you're currently climbing."

They rode in silence for a while, settling into their rhythm. Greg noticed how Mo maintained an unwavering pace, not too fast, not too slow. Despite the constant uphill, he never seemed to struggle.

"There are four types of business growth," Mo said as they approached the first switchback. "Vertical, horizontal, process, and financial. Each affects your cash flow differently."

The switchback required them to slow slightly, then accelerate again as they completed the turn.

"Vertical growth means serving the same customers with more services or products," Mo continued. "In your case, adding fertilizing, hedge trimming, or seasonal clean-up for existing clients."

"That seems easiest."

"It often is. You leverage existing relationships and infrastructure." Mo took a drink from his water bottle. "But it requires new skills and inventory. The cash flow impact is usually moderate. Some upfront investment but faster returns since you're selling to existing customers."

They passed a mile marker. Seven miles to go.

"Horizontal growth means more of the same, expanding your core service to more customers." Mo maintained his steady pace. "More lawns, more locations, more crews."

The gradient increased, forcing Greg to shift down again. Mo adjusted his gearing smoothly as Greg's sort of clunked awkwardly.

"The cash flow impact of horizontal growth is significant," Mo said. "Each new customer or location requires similar upfront costs. You're essentially replicating your model, which means replicating your cash needs."

The eastern sky was beginning to lighten, the first hints of dawn coloring the horizon.

"Process growth is about efficiency, serving the same customers better or at lower cost." Mo navigated around a pothole. "Better equipment, improved routing, streamlined operations."

"And what about the cash flow impact?" Greg showed genuine interest.

"Usually heavy upfront, with delayed returns. You're investing today for efficiency tomorrow." Mo shifted his weight slightly as the road steepened again. "But once the investment is absorbed, margins improve permanently."

"Can you give me a specific example for my lawn business?" Greg asked, adjusting his own gears to match the incline.

"Sure. Let's say you invest in a route optimization app that costs $500. That's a cash outflow today. But if it saves you fifteen minutes per client in travel time, and you service twenty-five clients weekly, that's over six hours saved. That's either six more clients you can service with the same labor cost, or six hours of labor cost you can eliminate."

Greg did the quick math. "So if I pay Samuel $15 an hour, that's $90 weekly savings, meaning the app pays for itself in about six weeks."

"It pays for itself! That's process growth. You haven't added new services or clients, but you've improved your margin structure permanently. Financial growth, the fourth type of growth, might involve renegotiating your vendor terms to get 45 days to pay instead of 30, improving your cash position without changing operations."

They reached another switchback, this one tighter than the first. As they made the turn, the road pitched up more severely.

"This is where the real climb starts," Mo said, shifting to a lower gear, standing on the pedals periodically. "Notice how we're gearing down? We're sacrificing speed for sustainability."

Greg followed suit, finding a gear that let him maintain cadence despite the steeper grade.

"Back to financial growth," Mo continued after they settled into the new rhythm. "This means improving margins, cash flow, and returns on investment without necessarily selling more."

"How do you do that? I mean, you mentioned vendor terms, but what else fits here?"

"Payment terms, pricing strategies, inventory management, debt restructuring. All the financial mechanics that affect how money flows through the business." Mo was breathing harder now but maintained his steady pace. "The cash flow impact varies, but it's often the most capital-efficient type of growth."

The road continued its relentless climb. Greg's legs were beginning to burn, but he was determined to keep up with Mo.

"So which type should I pursue?"

"That depends on your goals and constraints." Mo glanced over. "What's your biggest constraint right now?"

Greg thought about it. "Time, probably. I'm at capacity with twenty clients."

"And what's your goal?"

"More income, I guess. Maybe eventually make this my full-time job."

Mo gazed ahead as he considered his response. "Then you're looking at a combination of horizontal growth, which requires hiring, and financial growth to improve your margins."

They passed another mile marker. Still six miles to the summit.

"But here's the critical question," Mo said. "Does your current model scale?"

"What do you mean?"

"Can you multiply it profitably? Some businesses are inherently scalable. The systems and economics work better at larger size.

Others hit diminishing returns or even negative returns as they grow."

Greg frowned. "How do I know which type mine is?"

"By understanding your unit economics and operating leverage." Mo took another drink from his water bottle. "Unit economics means the profit contribution—often called the *contribution margin*—of each additional client. That is, how much money you keep from each new lawn you mow. Operating leverage is about spreading your fixed costs (like insurance and equipment payments) across more clients. The more clients share those fixed costs, the more profitable each one becomes."

The road curved again, revealing another series of switchbacks climbing higher up the mountain. The first rays of sun were now visible on the horizon, painting the clouds in brilliant golds and pinks.

"Let's break it down," Mo said. "What's your average revenue per client?"

"About a hundred dollars a month."

"And the direct costs to service each client? Gas, blade wear, time value?"

Greg calculated quickly. "Maybe thirty dollars."

"So your contribution margin is seventy dollars per client." Mo sat up in the saddle a bit, shifting his weight to get more comfortable. "Now, what are your fixed costs? The expenses you'd have whether you had one client or fifty?"

"Equipment payments, insurance, phone, website, accounting software… about six hundred a month."

"That means you need about nine clients just to cover fixed costs before you start earning profits." Mo navigated around another pothole. "Nine clients at seventy dollars each is six hundred

91

and thirty dollars, which covers—barely—your estimated fixed costs of six hundred a month. That's your breakeven point."

Greg had never analyzed his business quite this way before.

"Now," Mo continued, "the scalability question: If you hire someone to mow lawns, how does that change your unit economics?"

Greg thought about it. "I'd have labor costs for each client, which reduces the contribution margin."

"That's true. But you could service more clients, which spreads the fixed costs. The question is whether the trade-off is favorable." Mo shifted again as they approached another steep section. "This is why many small businesses hit growth plateaus. The economics of the next level don't work."

They rode in silence for a while, each focusing on the increasingly challenging climb. The sunrise was now in full glory, illuminating the valley below them in warm morning light.

"You know what makes this climb manageable?" Mo asked after they completed another switchback.

"What?"

"Consistent pacing." Mo gestured to his pedaling cadence. "Not too fast, not too slow. Business growth requires the same approach. Rush it, and you flame out. Too slow, and you never build momentum."

They passed the halfway point, four miles down, four to go. The gradient had become serious now, requiring their full attention and effort.

"The bikes we're riding today are purpose-built for climbing," Mo said between measured breaths. "Lightweight, appropriate gearing, efficient power transfer. Your business model needs the same intentional design if you want to scale successfully."

Greg was working hard now, finding it difficult to talk and climb simultaneously. Mo seemed to sense this and continued without expecting responses.

"When I decided to scale my landscaping business, I spent three months redesigning our service model. Changed our pricing structure, routing system, equipment configuration, and hiring profile." Mo maintained his steady cadence. "Many entrepreneurs try to scale a flawed model and wonder why they struggle."

Another mile marker passed. Three miles to go, and the steepest sections still ahead.

"The cash flow implications of scaling are where most businesses fail," Mo said. "Growth consumes cash, sometimes much more than owners anticipate."

"Why?" Greg managed to ask.

"New equipment, additional inventory, training costs, marketing expenses, larger facilities, all needed before the new revenue materializes." Mo took another drink from his water bottle. "Then there's the working capital to support larger operations. More accounts receivable, more payroll to cover, more supplies on hand."

The road narrowed and steepened considerably. They were forced to ride single file, Mo leading the way.

"This is where we separate preparation from aspiration," Mo called back. "Many start the climb, few complete it."

Greg's legs burned with the effort, but the high-end bike Mo had provided made a noticeable difference. The lightweight frame and precision components translated his effort into forward motion more efficiently than his old Schwinn ever could.

"Remember what I said about operating leverage?" Mo asked after they rounded another bend. "It works in both directions. More volume spreads fixed costs, improving margins. But if volume drops, those fixed costs become crushing."

Two miles to go. The switchbacks were tighter now, the road steeper. Greg shifted to his lowest gear, focusing entirely on maintaining forward motion.

"The most dangerous point in scaling," Mo called back, "is when you've committed to the higher fixed costs but haven't yet generated the additional revenue to support them. Many businesses run out of cash in that gap."

One more mile. The summit was visible now, a communications tower marking the highest point. The gradient was punishing, requiring every ounce of strength and technique they possessed.

"This is... definitely... a metaphor," Greg gasped.

Mo laughed despite the exertion. "The hardest part... right before... breakthrough."

They pushed on, the final half-mile seeming endless. Then suddenly, mercifully, the road leveled out as they reached the summit parking area. They rolled to a stop, unclipped from their pedals, and dismounted on legs that felt like rubber.

The view was spectacular. Miles of countryside spread out below them, bathed in the golden light of early morning. They could see neighboring towns, rivers, forests, all from a perspective impossible to obtain from below.

"This," Mo said when he caught his breath, "is the strategic view. You can't see this from the valley."

They walked their bikes to a picnic table and sat, drinking water and recovering from the effort.

"Scaling a business gives you the same perspective advantage," Mo continued. "You see opportunities and threats invisible to smaller operators. But you have to complete the climb to gain the view."

Greg just stared ahead, still too winded for much conversation.

"Now, about your lawn business," Mo said. "Let's talk about whether and how to scale it."

He pulled an energy bar from his pocket, broke it in half, and offered part to Greg.

"Based on what you've told me, you're at a classic growth decision point. Your current model works. It's profitable and cash-flow positive. But it's maxed out your personal capacity."

Greg chewed on his energy bar, indicating with a quick flick of his eyes that he understood.

"So you have three options," Mo held up his fingers one by one. "One, maintain current scale but improve profitability through price increases or efficiency. Two, hire help and expand horizontally. Three, add services to increase revenue per client."

"Or some combination," Greg suggested.

"Good thinking. But each requires a different cash strategy." Mo sipped his water. "For option one, you need minimal additional cash. For option two, you need working capital to cover payroll and additional equipment until new clients are onboarded. For option three, you need inventory and training investment."

Greg pulled out his notebook, his breathing finally returning to normal. "So how do I decide?"

"Start with your personal goals. Scaling isn't just about the business. It's about the life you want to build." Mo gestured to the expansive view. "What's your summit? What are you climbing toward?"

Greg hadn't thought about it quite that way before. "I guess I want financial security, flexibility, and eventually to build something valuable enough to sell or pass on."

"Good. Now we can work backward." Mo motioned for Greg's notebook, then took it and drew a simple diagram. "If the goal is to build value, you need a business that's not dependent on you personally. That means systems, team members, and repeatable processes."

He drew three ascending plateaus.

"Most service businesses go through these stages of scaling. First plateau is solo practitioner: you doing all the work. Second is small team: you plus a few others, with you still involved in operations. Third is true business: functioning without your daily involvement."

"I'm at the first plateau."

"Exactly. Moving to the second requires different skills and resources than what got you here." Mo tapped the page. "You've mastered technical skills, how to mow lawns efficiently. Now you need management skills, how to hire, train, and oversee others doing the work."

"And the cash flow implications?"

"Significant. The transition between plateaus is when businesses are most cash-vulnerable." Mo drew a dip between each plateau. "You're investing in the next level before fully realizing its benefits."

Greg looked out over the valley, thinking about the parallel between this mountain climb and the business journey ahead.

"So do I need to decide between horizontal growth or adding services?" he asked.

"Not necessarily. But you need to sequence them correctly from a cash perspective." Mo turned the page and sketched a timeline. "If I were advising you, I'd suggest this approach: First, implement a small price increase on existing clients, say 8%. That improves cash flow with minimal risk."

He drew a small bump on the timeline.

"Second, add one complementary service with high margins and low upfront investment, perhaps lawn edging or basic hedge trimming. Offer it to existing clients only." Another, larger bump appeared on the timeline.

"Third, use the improved cash flow to hire your first part-time helper for basic mowing. This frees you to handle the higher-value services and sales." A dip followed by a larger bump appeared on the timeline.

"Fourth, with more capacity, add five to seven new clients. Fifth, repeat the cycle. Another service addition, another part-time hire, more clients."

The timeline now showed a series of small dips followed by progressively larger increases.

"The key is that each step increases cash before you commit to the next investment." Mo handed the napkin to Greg. "This is staged scaling. Less dramatic than hiring three people at once, but much more cash-flow friendly."

Greg studied the timeline. "This makes sense. Each step builds on the previous one."

"It's like our climb today," Mo said, gesturing to the road they'd ascended. "We didn't sprint the first mile and burn out. We maintained a sustainable pace that got us all the way to the top."

As Greg stashed his trusty notebook, they packed away their water bottles and prepared for the descent.

"One more thing about scaling," Mo said as they clipped back into their pedals. "The skills that got you here won't get you there. Solo success requires technical excellence. Scaling requires systems thinking and leadership."

"Did you struggle with that transition?" Greg asked.

Mo laughed. "Mightily. I was the best landscaper in my company. Could edge a lawn perfectly, diagnose any irrigation issue, design beautiful plantings. But none of that mattered when I had fifteen employees. What mattered was whether I could create systems that allowed average performers to deliver consistent results."

They positioned their bikes at the summit road entrance, preparing for the descent.

"The descent is where we test everything," Mo said. "Our equipment, our judgment, our nerve. Scaling a business tests the same things. Ready?"

Greg smiled in agreement, feeling a mix of excitement and apprehension. The road down looked steeper from this vantage point than it had felt coming up.

"Follow my line, control your speed, and trust your equipment," Mo advised. "Just like in business growth. Follow a proven path, maintain control, and invest in the right tools."

With that, Mo pushed off, quickly picking up speed as gravity took hold. Greg followed, the high-performance bike responding instantly to his inputs. The first few turns were tense, but soon he found a rhythm, braking before corners and letting the bike run on straightaways.

The descent was exhilarating, covering in minutes what had taken hours to climb. The wind rushed past, the scenery blurred, and Greg felt a sense of both control and abandonment. He was working with forces much larger than himself, guiding rather than powering the bike.

When they reached the bottom, both were grinning despite the early morning chill.

"Now that," Mo said as they rolled to a stop at the parking area, "is the reward for a well-executed climb."

As they loaded the bikes onto Mo's rack, Greg reflected on the morning's lesson.

"So scaling isn't always the right answer?"

"It's the right answer when it serves your goals and when your model supports it." Mo secured the bikes. "But timing and execution matter just as much as the decision itself."

"And cash flow is the limiting factor?"

"Almost always." Mo closed the tailgate. "Most business failures during scaling aren't from lack of sales or operational problems. They're from running out of cash during the transition between plateaus."

Greg made a note in his book:

Scale in stages, ensuring each stage generates cash before committing to the next.

"For next time," Mo said as they prepared to leave, "I want you to draft a staged scaling plan with specific cash flow projections for each step. What investments are required? How long until positive returns? What contingencies do you need?"

"Will do." Greg tucked his notebook away. "Thanks for today, Uncle Mo. The climb was tough, but the view was worth it."

"Always is." Mo smiled. "In business and in life, the best perspectives come after the hardest climbs."

As Greg drove home, his legs sore but his mind energized, he thought about the parallels between the morning's ride and the business journey ahead. The steady pace required for sustainable progress. The appropriate equipment for the challenge. The strategic perspective gained only by reaching new heights.

Most importantly, he understood that scaling wasn't a single decision but a series of coordinated steps, each building on the one before. Just as they had climbed the mountain one switchback at a time, he would grow his business one stage at a time, always with an eye on the cash flow implications of each move.

When he arrived home, Greg spread his financial projections across the kitchen table. For the first time, he looked beyond the current month and quarter, sketching out a two-year growth trajectory with the staged approach Mo had outlined.

The immediate next steps Mo had hinted at became all the more clear: a modest price increase, followed by adding edging services for existing clients, then hiring Samuel as part-time help. Each step calculated not just for profitability but for its cash flow timing.

His father walked through the kitchen, pausing when he saw the timeline Greg had drawn out with projected revenue milestones and staffing decisions.

"Two-year projections?" his father asked, setting down his keys.

"Mo calls it 'climbing the mountain in stages,'" Greg replied, pointing to his notes. "Each step has to be timed right. You can't hire help until you have consistent revenue to support them, but you can't grow revenue without eventually getting help."

His father studied the progression Greg had mapped out. "And you're factoring in the cash flow lag between service expansion and payment collection?"

"Yeah, that's why the edging services come first. Same clients, faster payment, builds cash reserves before I take on payroll risk."

His father nodded slowly, pulling out a chair. "Show me how you calculated the breakeven point for adding an employee."

This wasn't just about getting bigger. It was about climbing higher while maintaining balance and control. The summit was within reach, not in a single sprint, but through steady, purposeful ascent.

WEATHERING THE STORM

FALL HAD ARRIVED in earnest. Greg's lawn care business had been operating for five months now, following the staged growth plan Mo had helped him develop. He'd raised prices modestly, added edging services, and hired Samuel, a part-time helper who handled basic mowing while Greg focused on client relationships and higher-margin services. Instead of just a side hustle, it had become his day job, and more.

The business now served twenty-seven clients, a manageable increase that had boosted revenue without overwhelming their capacity. Cash flow remained positive, with enough reserves to cover two weeks of operations if revenue suddenly stopped.

But on this particular Thursday morning, Greg stared at his weather app with growing concern. A major storm system was approaching, promising three days of heavy rain and strong winds. Already, clients were calling to reschedule. Three days of lost work meant three days of lost revenue, with wages and overhead continuing regardless.

Greg called Mo.

"I see you've been checking the forecast too," Mo said by way of greeting.

"Three days of rain. Maybe more," Greg replied. "I've built some reserves like you taught me, but this will be the first real test."

"Sounds like perfect timing for our next lesson. Meet me at Silver Creek in an hour."

"The stream that runs through Westside Park? Why there?"

"You'll see." Mo hung up.

Silver Creek was normally a placid waterway that meandered through one of the city's largest parks. Today, however, it was already rising, the usually clear water turned muddy brown by runoff from early rain.

Mo was waiting on the footbridge that spanned the widest section, watching the accelerating current below.

"What do you see?" Mo asked as Greg joined him.

Greg looked down at the swelling creek. "Water rising. Getting faster."

"And if you were responsible for this park, what would you be thinking about right now?"

Greg considered the question. "Probably flood control. Whether the bridges and paths can handle the overflow."

"That's what I would say. Every business faces storms. Some predictable, like seasonal slowdowns. Others unexpected, like economic downturns or supply chain disruptions. The question isn't if they'll come, but how you'll handle them when they do."

They watched as a branch swept beneath them, carried rapidly by the strengthening current.

"Financial crises in business come in three forms," Mo continued. "Revenue shocks, expense spikes, and liquidity crunches. Sometimes all three at once."

"Like this storm," Greg said. "Revenue drops because we can't work, expenses continue, and cash flow takes a hit."

"Precisely. But here's the thing about storms. You usually get warning signs." Mo gestured to the darkening sky. "You've been watching the forecast. You know what's coming. The question is whether you've prepared appropriately."

A light rain began to fall, and they moved to a nearby gazebo that offered shelter. From this vantage point, they could still see the creek as it continued to rise.

"Let me tell you about the worst financial storm I ever faced," Mo said, settling onto a bench. "It was my seventh year in the landscaping business. We had forty employees, multiple crews, significant equipment investments, and a healthy client list that included several large commercial properties."

Greg sat across from him, notebook ready. Outside, the creek's waters had turned from clear to muddy brown, carrying small branches and debris.

"That August, we faced a perfect storm, literally and figuratively," Mo continued. "First, record rainfall caused nearly three weeks of work delays. Second, our largest client declared bankruptcy, leaving a $45,000 invoice unpaid. Third, two of our major pieces of equipment failed within days of each other, requiring expensive emergency repairs."

"All at once?" Greg winced. "What did you do first?"

"First, I panicked," Mo admitted with a wry smile. "For about an hour. Then I pulled myself together and implemented what I now call the Storm Protocol, a systematic approach to financial crisis management."

The rain intensified, drumming on the gazebo roof. Greg glanced outside, where park workers had arrived, wearing ponchos, and begun placing sandbags along sections of the creek bank.

"Let me tell you about the Storm Protocol," Mo said, as they watched the creek rising. "In cycling, experienced riders have a specific approach to handling unexpected hazards on the trail: fallen trees, sudden washouts, or mechanical failures. There are three phases: Immediate Response, Damage Assessment, and Adaptive Completion."

"How does that translate to business?"

"The first phase is Immediate Protection," Mo explained. "When a cyclist encounters an obstacle like a fallen tree blocking the trail, they don't try to immediately remove the entire tree. They first secure their own safety, assess immediate hazards, and find the most critical path through."

Greg's face told Mo that he understood. "In business, that means preserving cash reserves and taking immediate action to prevent further damage."

"You got it. You're not trying to solve everything at once. You're directing resources to the most critical areas." Mo watched park workers placing sandbags along the creek. "Just like they're doing now, protecting the most essential infrastructure first."

Greg's phone buzzed. A text from Samuel: *Hey boss, should I still come in tomorrow with this storm?*

Greg looked up at Mo uncertainly. "Speaking of immediate protection… That's Samuel asking about tomorrow."

"What's your instinct?" Mo asked.

Greg stared at his phone, weighing the options. "If I tell him not to come, I save on wages. But if the rain stops earlier than forecast…"

"There's your first crisis decision," Mo said. "No perfect answer, just trade-offs."

Greg typed back: *Let's touch base in the morning. If it's still pouring, we'll reschedule. If it clears, we'll hit the priority clients.*

"Hedging your bet?" Mo asked, glimpsing at the message.

"Trying to," Greg replied, tucking his phone away. "Preserving cash without losing opportunity."

"Not bad," Mo shifted his weight. "What else besides managing expenses is part of Immediate Protection?"

"Communication, I'm guessing?" Greg ventured. "I should probably text clients, too."

"Bingo. Communication is critical. I immediately called every client, vendor, and employee to explain the situation. No sugar-coating, just honesty about the challenges and my plan to address them.

"Were people understanding?" Greg asked.

"Most were. Some weren't." Mo shrugged. "But all of them appreciated the transparency. Nothing destroys confidence faster than silence during a crisis."

The creek had risen further, water now lapping at the footbridge where they'd stood earlier. A park worker was taking photos and making notes on a clipboard.

"See that?" Mo pointed. "She's moved to phase two, Damage Assessment. In business, this happens days three through seven of a crisis."

Thunder rumbled in the distance. Greg shifted in his seat, thinking about his own business. "So how exactly do you assess damage in a business crisis?"

"With data, not emotion," Mo replied, his tone firm. "You need to update your cash flow projection daily, track canceled orders, delayed payments, unexpected expenses. All of it."

"Sounds overwhelming when you're already dealing with the immediate problems," Greg observed.

"It is. That's why most people do it poorly or skip it entirely." Mo leaned forward. "But this assessment is critical because it helps you distinguish between temporary and permanent damage."

"What's the difference?"

"Temporary damage is recoverable. Postponed services can be rescheduled, delayed cash flow will eventually arrive. Like those paths…" Mo gestured to the flooded walking paths. "They're underwater now but will be usable again when the water recedes."

Greg's posture changed as comprehension dawned. "And permanent damage?"

"Anything that's structurally changed or lost forever." Mo pointed to a small footbridge that had partially collapsed under the force of the water. "Like that. It's not coming back without significant reconstruction."

As if on cue, the rain intensified again, sending a fresh surge of water into the creek.

"What about your landscaping crisis?" Greg asked. "What was temporary versus permanent?"

"The rain delays were temporary; we could make up most of that work later. The equipment repairs were a temporary cash flow hit." Mo's expression darkened slightly. "But the bankrupt client? That was permanent damage; that $45,000 was never coming back."

"So that brings us to the third phase," Greg prompted, watching as park workers began roping off the damaged areas.

"Strategic Reconstruction. This is where most businesses fail during crisis recovery." Mo traced a diagram in Greg's notebook, three overlapping circles. "They either try to return to exactly how things were before, or they overreact and change everything. Both approaches typically fail."

Greg studied the diagram. "So what works?"

"Targeted adaptation based on what the crisis revealed." Mo tapped the outer circle. "First, strengthen obvious vulnerabilities." He moved to the middle circle. "Second, preserve and possibly expand core strengths." Finally, he pointed to the center. "Third, strategically abandon areas that the crisis proved unsustainable."

Outside, the park director had arrived and was giving directions to the workers, some continuing to place sandbags, others beginning to clear debris from drainage areas.

"Can you give me a specific example from your landscaping crisis?" Greg asked, watching the coordinated response outside.

Looking where Greg looked, Mo continued. "When our big client went bankrupt, it revealed our dangerous exposure to a few large customers. During reconstruction, we diversified our client base and implemented stricter credit policies. That was addressing a vulnerability."

"Did you have to let people go?" Greg asked, thinking about his own part-time helper, Samuel.

"We reduced hours temporarily but didn't lay anyone off," Mo replied. "That was a conscious choice, part of preserving our core strength, which was our trained team."

"And what did you abandon?"

"Our high-end landscape design services." Mo shrugged. "The crisis showed they were too capital-intensive and had inconsistent margins. We scaled that division back significantly and eventually spun it off."

The rain had begun to ease slightly, though the creek remained swollen and rapid.

"Now, let's apply this to your lawn care business and the current situation," Mo said, turning the conversation to Greg's immediate challenge. "What would your Immediate Protection plan look like for the next 48 hours?"

Greg thought for a moment. "Preserve cash. Postpone any non-essential purchases. Communicate with clients to reschedule services. And... I guess make sure our equipment is stored safely so it doesn't get damaged in the storm."

"Good start. What about Samuel's hours?"

Greg frowned. "That's tougher. I don't want to shortchange him, but I'm not bringing in revenue for these rain days."

"This is where advance planning matters." Mo tapped the notebook. "Did you build rain day contingencies into your pricing and reserves?"

"Some, but maybe not enough for a three-day storm."

"Then you have a decision to make. You can either reduce his hours and preserve cash or maintain his hours and accept the hit to your reserves." Mo's gaze was steady. "There's no universally right answer. It depends on your priorities and runway."

Greg made some quick calculations. "I think I can keep him at full hours for this storm. We have enough reserves. But if it extended to a week..."

"You'd need a different approach," Mo finished. "That's crisis management. Different responses for different severity levels."

They watched as the creek continued to rise, water now flowing with significant force around the footbridge supports.

"Now, what would your Damage Assessment look like after the storm passes?" Mo asked.

Greg thought about it. "I'd need to calculate precisely how much revenue we lost, what expenses continued during the downtime, and the net impact on cash reserves."

"Don't forget opportunity costs," Mo added. "Potential new clients you couldn't meet with, estimates you couldn't provide, seasonal services you missed the window for."

110

"Opportunity costs. Interesting." Greg pondered the significance of those words and then reached for his notebook.

"Then comes Strategic Reconstruction. You analyze what the crisis revealed about your business model." Mo's tone grew more serious. "Does your pricing adequately account for weather disruptions? Is your client mix diversified enough? Are your fixed costs too high relative to your variable revenue?"

The rain had continued to ease, though the creek remained swollen and rapid. Greg glanced up at Mo but then kept writing.

"Let me share three specific cash flow strategies for crisis management," Mo continued. "First, the Cash Acceleration Strategy."

He reached for Greg's notebook, and Greg handed it to him. Mo turned to a blank page and drew a timeline. "In a crisis, accelerate all inflows and delay all outflows, ethically and without damaging relationships. Offer discounts for immediate payment. Extend payables where possible. Convert inventory or unused assets to cash."

"Wouldn't discounts reduce my total revenue?"

"Yes, but in a crisis, timing often matters more than total." Mo tapped the paper. "A 5% discount that brings cash in today might be worth more than full payment in 30 days if having that cash prevents a larger problem."

Greg took his notebook back from Mo, finished his note, then flipped to a fresh page and handed it back to Mo.

"Second strategy: Segmented Preservation." Mo drew three concentric circles. "It's like triage. Decide what to save first when you can't save everything. Not all parts of your business have equal value during a crisis. The inner circle represents essential operations, the absolute minimum required to survive, like maintaining your core clients and basic equipment. The middle

111

circle is important but flexible components, like marketing or office upgrades. The outer circle is everything else, the nice-to-haves you can live without temporarily. Or even permanently in some cases."

"And you protect from the inside out?"

"Yes! In severe crises, sacrifice the outer circle completely to protect the core. In moderate crises, reduce the middle circle while completely preserving the core."

Outside, the park authorities had closed several secondary paths to focus on protecting the main pavilion and primary walkways, a real-world demonstration of Mo's principle.

"The third strategy is Relationship Banking." Mo's looked serious. "In a true crisis, your relationships become your most valuable currency. Suppliers who will extend terms. Clients who will pay early. Employees who will work flexible hours. Lenders who will restructure payments. But you have to work at building those relationships. Make them strong before you need them."

"How do you do that?"

"By depositing in the relational bank when times are good." Mo smiled slightly. "Pay suppliers early when you can. Deliver extra value to clients as often as possible. Support employees during their personal challenges. Maintain perfect communication with lenders."

Greg absorbed what Mo was saying, thinking about his own business relationships.

"Remember my landscaping crisis? We survived largely because of relationship banking," Mo continued. "Our equipment supplier extended our terms from 30 to 90 days. Several loyal clients prepaid for future services. Our bank restructured our equipment loans without penalties."

"They helped because you'd built good relationships?"

"I'd built *great* relationships. That's the difference between survival and failure when the storm hits hardest." Mo glanced at his watch. "Now, let's get practical about your current situation."

For the next hour, they worked through specific scenarios for Greg's business, calculating the impact of the current storm and developing contingency plans for potentially worse situations: a week of rain, equipment failure during peak season, the loss of a major client.

By the time they finished, the rain had slowed to a drizzle, though the creek remained high and fast.

"There's one more aspect of crisis management I need to share," Mo said as they prepared to leave. "It's perhaps the most important but often overlooked."

"What's that?"

"Crisis reveals character, both personal and organizational." Mo appeared thoughtful. "How you respond when things are at their worst defines you more clearly than all your actions when things are going well."

They stepped out of the gazebo, carefully navigating around puddles and minor flooding.

"During my landscaping crisis, I made a commitment that we would maintain quality for existing clients even while cutting costs elsewhere. I personally called every client to explain our situation and assure them our work wouldn't suffer." Mo paused at the edge of the park. "That decision cost us short-term cash flow but preserved our reputation, which proved invaluable during recovery."

"It was the right call?" Greg thought he knew, but he asked anyway.

"For us, yes. Every business needs to decide its own crisis principles." Mo looked back at the receding creek. "But here's what

I've learned: the businesses that emerge strongest from crises are those that stay true to their core values while being flexible about almost everything else."

As they reached the parking lot, Mo turned to Greg one last time.

"For next week, I want you to further develop what we've been working on and show me a complete Storm Protocol for your business. Not just for weather disruptions, but for any potential crisis. Equipment failure, personal injury, economic downturn, loss of key clients."

"I'll keep working on it," Greg promised.

"Good. Because here's the paradox of crisis management. When you're thoroughly prepared for a crisis, you're less likely to experience one." Mo smiled. "The very act of planning reduces your vulnerability."

Greg drove home through puddle-strewn streets, thinking about Mo's Storm Protocol. The systematic approach made crisis management feel less overwhelming, more methodical. Immediate Protection. Damage Assessment. Strategic Reconstruction. Each phase with clear priorities and actions.

He thought about his lawn care business, its strengths, vulnerabilities, and relationships. The storm would pass, but others would come. The question wasn't if, but when and how severe. With proper planning, he could weather virtually any financial challenge.

That evening, Greg created a Storm Protocol document for his business. He identified core operations that must be protected at all costs. He listed relationship-banking opportunities to develop. He even drafted crisis communication templates for clients, suppliers, and his part-time help.

As he worked, the rain continued outside, but its sound no longer brought anxiety. Instead, it reminded him of Mo's words at the creek: "The question isn't if storms will come, but how you'll handle them when they do."

His business now had an answer to that question, a systematic approach to crisis that would preserve the core while positioning for eventual recovery. Financial storms, like weather systems, would always be part of the landscape. But with proper preparation, they could be managed, navigated, and sometimes even leveraged for stronger future growth.

Growing up, whenever he left the house, Greg's dad used to say, *"Acuérdate quién eres." Remember who you are.* Thinking through Mo's counsel, his Dad's daily reminder echoed in his mind.

Greg added a final note to his Storm Protocol:

In crisis, preserve cash, protect relationships, and remember that how you respond defines who you are.

THE SCENIC ROUTE

WINTER CREPT IN. Greg's lawn care business had naturally slowed with the season, though he'd added leaf removal and basic winter cleanup services that kept some revenue flowing. Following Mo's guidance, he'd built sufficient reserves during the busy months to weather this predictable slowdown.

Most importantly, Greg had begun thinking differently about his business. What had started as a side hustle to make extra money had evolved into something more meaningful: a vehicle for creating value, solving problems, and potentially building long-term wealth.

The phone rang early Saturday morning. Mo, of course.

"Got plans today?" Mo asked without preamble.

"Just some paperwork for the business. Why?"

"Put it aside. I'm taking you on the scenic route."

"Another bike ride?" Greg asked, remembering their previous lessons on two wheels.

"Not exactly. The trails are snowy, and those skinny bike tires won't cut it. Be ready in thirty minutes. Dress warm."

When Mo arrived, he was driving not his usual truck but a pristine vintage Jeep CJ7. Its forest green paint gleamed despite the winter morning frost.

"Jeep hair, don't care!" Greg joked, climbing in. "But it's pretty chilly today to go topless?"

"You'll be fine," Mo groaned. "Needed something with four-wheel drive today. We're going exploring."

They drove out of town, heading toward the foothills that rose to the west. The morning was clear and cold, the landscape transformed by a light dusting of snow that had fallen overnight.

"Today's about long-term planning," Mo said as they left the city behind. "There are two ways to approach the future—the direct route and the scenic route."

Greg watched the landscape around him go by as the suburban sprawl gave way to rural countryside.

"Most business owners take the direct route. They set financial targets, create step-by-step plans to reach them, then execute with tunnel vision." Mo navigated a winding road that began to climb into the hills. "There's nothing wrong with that approach. It's efficient. Often effective. But it misses something important."

"What's that?"

"Context. Perspective. Alternative possibilities." Mo turned onto a narrower road, this one unpaved. "The scenic route takes longer, but shows you things you'd never see otherwise."

Mo's Jeep handled the increasingly rough terrain with ease, climbing steadily as the trees thickened around them. After about twenty minutes on the unpaved road, Mo pulled over at a small turnout.

"First stop," he announced. "You'll wanna leave your jacket on."

They exited the vehicle and walked a short path through the trees, emerging at a clearing that offered a stunning panoramic view. The entire valley spread out below them, the city visible in the distance, surrounded by farmland, suburbs, forested areas, industrial zones, and transportation corridors.

"What do you see?" Mo asked, his standard opening question.

Greg surveyed the landscape. "Everything. The whole region."

"The strategic view." Mo looked around, taking it all in. "Most business owners never see this perspective. They're too close to their operations, too focused on the next quarter or the next sale."

"Not to sound cliché," Greg glanced around at trees behind them, "but not seeing the forest for the trees?"

"Exactly." Mo pointed to various features in the landscape. "Look at how everything connects. The highways feeding the industrial zone. The neighborhoods surrounding commercial areas. The agricultural belt providing a buffer between developed regions."

Greg studied the pattern, seeing the logic in the regional development.

"Long-term planning requires this perspective," Mo continued. "Not just seeing your business but understanding its place in the larger ecosystem. Economic trends, demographic shifts, technological changes, regulatory environments."

"It's hard to think that broadly when you're just trying to make payroll, "Greg offered.

"*¡Claro que sí!* That's why most small businesses stay small." Mo turned to face Greg. "But if you want to build something truly valuable, you need to make time for the scenic route. The strategic perspective that reveals opportunities and threats invisible from ground level."

They returned to the CJ and continued their journey, the road narrowing further as they climbed higher. The trees occasionally opened to reveal glimpses of the valley below, now from an even more elevated vantage point.

"The P&L, the balance sheet, cash flow management. Those are all tactical tools," Mo said as they drove. "Essential for day-to-day operations and near-term planning. But long-term success requires strategic thinking that goes beyond financial statements."

"Strategic thinking?"

"Yes. Strategic thinking is not the same as tactical thinking. First, you need to understand the difference between goals and systems," Mo replied. "Goals are outcomes you want to achieve. Specific revenue targets, number of clients, profit margins. Systems are the processes that lead to those outcomes."

"Like the difference between wanting to summit Mountain View Road in less than an hour and establishing a training regimen to achieve it?" Greg mused.

"Perfect analogy." Mo smiled approvingly. "Most business owners obsess over goals but underinvest in systems. The irony is that systems are far more important for long-term success."

The road took a sharp turn, and Mo slowed and adjusted his angle to navigate a particularly rough section, operating the CJ with the same skill and finesse Greg had seen him use on his mountain bike.

"When I built my landscaping business, I discovered this truth the hard way," he continued. "My first two years, I focused exclusively on revenue goals. Worked sixteen-hour days, took on any client willing to pay, cut corners on processes. Hit my targets but created a mess."

"What happened?"

"Burnout, inconsistent quality, cash flow chaos." Mo shook his head at the memory. "Year three, I shifted my focus to systems. Client selection processes, standardized operations, financial controls, team development frameworks. Revenue growth actually slowed initially, but profitability improved dramatically. By year five, we were growing faster than ever, but with vastly less stress."

They reached another turnout, this one smaller and unmarked. Mo parked the Jeep and they exited, following a barely visible trail through dense pines. After a five-minute hike, they emerged at a rocky outcropping that offered a different view. Not of the valley they'd left behind, but of the mountain range extending before them, peak after snow-dusted peak stretching to the horizon.

"Second stop," Mo announced. "The horizon view."

Greg stood beside him, taking in the magnificent vista.

"This perspective represents the second element of long-term planning: understanding time horizons," Mo said. "Most businesses operate with compressed time horizons. The next week, the next month, maybe the next quarter."

"Because that's what's urgent."

"Sure, it's front of mind, but building significant value requires thinking across multiple time horizons simultaneously." Mo pointed to the nearest peaks, then to the middle distance, then to the furthest visible mountains. "I think of these as one-year, three-year, and ten-year horizons."

Greg pulled out his notebook, feeling an important lesson forming.

"The key to effective long-term planning is making decisions that serve multiple time horizons," Mo continued. "Poor businesses sacrifice long-term value for short-term gain. Average businesses balance the two. Great businesses find strategies that serve both simultaneously."

"Can you give me an example?"

"Sure. When I was scaling my landscaping business, we faced a decision about equipment purchases." Mo sat on a flat rock, inviting Greg to join him. "The short-term, cost-efficient choice was to buy mid-range equipment, adequate for current needs and easier on cash flow. The long-term choice was premium equipment. More reliable, more efficient, longer-lasting, but much more expensive upfront."

"What did you do?"

"Neither. We developed a third option, a phased investment strategy combining strategic leasing and targeted ownership." Mo smiled as he thought about it. "We leased the most specialized equipment that we used less frequently. We purchased premium versions of our core, daily-use equipment. And we bought used but reliable versions of everything else."

"Serving multiple time horizons."

"Correct. The strategy preserved cash flow in the short term while building equity and efficiency for the long term." Mo gestured toward the layered mountain ranges. "Each decision considered impacts across all those horizons."

They sat in silence for a few minutes, absorbing the expansive view. A hawk circled lazily overhead, riding thermal currents in its patient search for prey.

"The third element of long-term planning is perhaps the most overlooked," Mo said eventually. "It's what I call trajectory thinking."

"What's that?"

"Understanding that success isn't about where you are now, but which direction you're moving and at what speed." Mo picked up a pinecone and tossed it over the edge, watching it bounce down the slope. "Two businesses can have identical current metrics. Same revenue, same profit, same customer count. But they can have wildly different values based on their trajectories."

The hawk suddenly dove, disappearing into the trees below, then reappeared moments later, something clutched in its talons.

"Nature understands trajectory," Mo noted, watching the bird. "The hawk doesn't strike where the prey is, but where it will be. Business works the same way."

They hiked back to the Jeep and continued their journey. The road now began to level out, having reached a high plateau. Mo followed what appeared to be a logging track, the vehicle swaying gently as it navigated the uneven terrain.

"Let me tell you how trajectory thinking saved my business during a major market shift," Mo said as they drove. "Around my eighth or ninth year, we faced a severe regional drought. Water restrictions were implemented, and suddenly, maintaining lush green lawns became politically incorrect and prohibitively expensive."

"That sounds like an existential threat for a landscaping business."

"It certainly could have been. Many of our competitors doubled down on fighting the trend, lobbying against restrictions, promoting workarounds, or just hoping the situation would improve." Mo navigated over a fallen branch. "But their trajectory was clearly negative, regardless of their current profitability."

"What did you do differently?"

"We completely repositioned our business around the trend rather than against it. Launched a 'Drought-Smart Landscapes' division that specialized in xeriscaping, native plants, and water-efficient irrigation systems." Mo beamed as he thought about it. "Within eighteen months, it grew to represent over sixty percent of our business. Within three years, competitors who hadn't adapted were bankrupt."

"You saw the trajectory and adjusted course."

"I had to. While they were defending their current position, we were building toward the inevitable future." Mo slowed as they approached a clearing. "Which brings us to our final stop."

Mo's CJ emerged from the trees into a breathtaking alpine meadow. Despite the winter season, it retained a rugged beauty, golden grasses poking through the light snow, framed by towering pines and distant peaks. Mo parked, and they walked to the center of the meadow.

"This is what we call the destination view," Mo said, turning slowly to take in the 360-degree panorama. "But here's the paradox of long-term planning: the most valuable destinations are rarely the ones you initially envision."

Greg listened, feeling the quiet significance of the moment.

"When I started my landscaping business, I had a clear ten-year plan," Mo continued. "Specific growth targets, expansion strategies, even an exit strategy to sell to a regional competitor. Practically none of it happened as planned."

"I don't understand. By then, I'm sure you had dialed in your contribution margins and breakeven points. And I bet your cash flow forecasts were on point. What went wrong?"

"Nothing went wrong. Reality happened." Mo smiled. "New opportunities emerged that I couldn't have anticipated. Market shifts required strategic pivots. Personal priorities evolved as I matured."

"So long-term planning is pointless?"

"Not at all. Long-term planning is essential, but not for the reasons most people think." Mo placed a hand on Greg's shoulder. "The value isn't in creating a perfect roadmap to a predetermined destination. It's in developing the strategic thinking muscles that let you navigate effectively regardless of how the landscape changes."

They walked the perimeter of the meadow, breath visible in the cold air.

"I eventually sold my landscaping business," Mo said, "but not to the competitor I'd originally envisioned. Instead, I developed an employee ownership plan and transitioned the company to my management team over a five-year period."

"Why the change in exit strategy?"

"By that point, I'd come to value legacy over maximizing sale price. I wanted the business culture we'd built to continue, wanted the team members who'd helped build it to benefit directly." Mo shrugged. "My values had evolved. My understanding of 'success' had matured. The scenic route showed me possibilities I couldn't see when I started."

They completed their circuit of the meadow and returned to the Jeep. As they settled in for the drive back, Mo turned to Greg.

"Now, let's talk about your lawn care business through these three lenses: systematic thinking, multiple time horizons, and trajectory assessment."

For the next hour, as they made their way back down the mountain, Mo guided Greg through a series of questions about his business. Not the tactical cash flow and operational issues they'd addressed in previous lessons, but bigger, more fundamental questions:

What systems, not just goals, was Greg developing? How were his decisions impacting one-year, three-year, and ten-year horizons? What trajectories—industry trends, customer preferences, technological changes—would shape his market in the coming years?

By the time they reached the main road, Greg had filled several pages with notes, diagrams, and strategic insights, messy and nearly illegible from the bumpy terrain Mo had navigated flawlessly.

"For our final exercise," Mo said as they approached the city limits, "I want you to create a three-horizon plan for your business."

"What does that look like?"

"First horizon: next twelve months. Specific, actionable steps with clear metrics and cash flow projections." Mo slowed to navigate a traffic circle. "Second horizon: one to three years. Strategic initiatives, capability development, and market positioning. Less specific on tactics, more focused on direction and milestones. I want you to really imagine what your company will look like. Describe it in as much detail as you can."

"And the third horizon?"

"Three to ten years. This isn't about specific targets but about the kind of business you want to build. Its values, its impact, its role in your life, and its place in the market." Mo turned onto Greg's street. "The three horizons should align and reinforce each other, not compete."

As they pulled up to Greg's house, Mo had one final thought to share.

"The scenic route takes longer. It has unexpected turns and occasional rough patches. Sometimes you wonder if you're lost." He put the Jeep in neutral and pulled the emergency brake, the familiar clicking from the handle reverberating in their ears. "But it reveals perspectives you can't get any other way and often leads to destinations far better than those you originally planned."

Greg gathered his notebook and prepared to exit. "Thanks, Uncle Mo. This was… different from our other lessons. Less technical, more philosophical."

"As it should be. Financial management is both science and art. Cash flow mechanics are the science. Essential, but ultimately just tools. The art is in how you use those tools to build something meaningful over time."

As Greg watched the Jeep drive away, he reflected on the journey they'd taken. Not just today's mountain expedition, but the months of lessons that had transformed his understanding of business.

He'd started with a simple desire to make extra money mowing lawns. Now he was thinking about systems development, multi-horizon planning, and trajectory analysis. From tactical cash management, Mo had gradually elevated his perspective to strategic value creation.

That evening, Greg started drafting his three-horizon plan. The first horizon came easily—specific growth targets, service additions, and operational improvements for the coming year. The second horizon required more thought but took shape as a vision of expanded services, streamlined systems, and perhaps a second full-time employee.

The third horizon proved the most challenging and the most revealing. As Greg projected seven to ten years forward, he found himself considering questions beyond business metrics. What kind of life did he want? What impact did he want his business to have on clients, the community, the environment? What would "success" mean beyond financial returns?

To his surprise, the answers that emerged weren't what he might have anticipated when he started his lawn business. He found himself sketching a vision not of a large landscaping operation with dozens of employees, but of a specialized, reputation-based business focused on sustainable landscape management, with technology integration and educational components.

As Mo had suggested, the scenic route revealed destinations he hadn't initially considered, possibilities that aligned more authentically with his evolving values and strengths.

Greg added a quote to the top of his three-horizon plan:

The scenic route takes longer but reveals better destinations.

He was beginning to understand that cash flow management—the focus of their initial lessons—wasn't just about keeping a business solvent. It was about creating the freedom and stability to make choices based on value rather than necessity. It was about building a vehicle that could take the scenic route by choice, not just the direct route by requirement.

The tactical tools Mo had taught him—P&L analysis, balance sheet management, cash flow projections—were essential. But their true purpose was now clearer than ever: to create the foundation for something more meaningful than mere survival or even short-term profitability.

They were building blocks for a business that could evolve, adapt, and ultimately reflect its owner's highest aspirations, not just his immediate needs.

THE RETURN JOURNEY

ONE YEAR HAD passed since Greg called and shown up at Mo's garage door, seeking advice about his lawn care business idea. What began as a simple side hustle had evolved into a thriving operation with thirty-five clients, two part-time employees, and a clear growth strategy. More importantly, Greg had developed a financial fluency that transformed how he viewed business and opportunities.

He sat at his kitchen table, reviewing his company's financial statements. The P&L showed healthy profitability. The Balance Sheet reflected growing equity and strategic asset allocation. The Cash Flow Statement confirmed strong liquidity with reserves for both opportunities and challenges.

But the numbers told only part of the story. Behind the figures lay a deeper understanding, a way of thinking Mo had cultivated through their monthly lessons.

His father appeared with his morning coffee, no longer surprised to find Greg immersed in financial analysis. What had once been an unusual Saturday night occurrence had become Greg's routine.

"How's the business looking?" his father asked, settling into the chair across from him.

"Better than I projected," Greg replied, turning his laptop screen toward his father. "We're ahead of plan on revenue, and the cash flow timing is exactly what Mo helped me predict."

His father studied the statements for several minutes, his expression thoughtful. Finally, he looked up at Greg.

"You know, when you first started working with Mo, I thought..." He paused, choosing his words carefully. "I thought he was teaching you shortcuts. But this..." he gestured toward the comprehensive financial analysis "This has a sort of sophisticated simplicity. An elegance even. And though it's simple, it's not simplistic. And practical. It's probably more useful than anything I learned in business school."

Greg looked up, surprised by the admission.

"What Mo has taught you isn't altogether unconventional," his father continued. "But it's more approachable this way. He taught you to understand the story behind the numbers, not just how to calculate them. That's harder to learn than formulas." He took a sip of his coffee. "I think maybe I owe you both a congratulations. Maybe even an apology."

"Nah Dad. Nothing to apologize for. Your dinnertime rants laid a great foundation that Mo just built on. I'm pretty lucky to have both of you." Their eyes locked, and they said more with their eyes in the moment that followed than any conversation would have.

Snapping him back to the moment, Greg's phone buzzed: *One year anniversary. Let's celebrate. Breakfast at Hilltop Café, 7 a.m. tomorrow.*

The following morning, Greg arrived at the café to find Mo already seated by the window, watching the sunrise paint the sky in brilliant oranges and pinks. Two steaming *cortaditos* waited on the table.

"Good morning, Greggo." Mo pushed one mug toward him. "How's it feel to be a year into your entrepreneurial journey?"

Greg sat, wrapping his hands around the warm mug. "Honestly? Nothing like I expected."

"In good ways or bad?"

"Mostly good. The business is doing well. Better than my projections. But it's more than that." Greg searched for the right words. "I see things differently now. Not just my business, but everything. Opportunities, challenges, even how I manage my personal finances."

Mo couldn't hide the teacher's satisfaction in his expression. "Financial literacy changes your perspective. It's like getting glasses after years of blurry vision. Suddenly, you see patterns and possibilities that were always there but invisible to you."

The waitress brought their breakfast, a simple fare of eggs, toast, fresh fruit, and, of course, crispy bacon. As they ate, Greg reflected on the year's lessons.

"You know what surprises me most?" he said between bites. "How everything connects. When we started, I thought each lesson—P&L, Balance Sheet, Cash Flow—was separate. But now I see they're different angles on the same reality."

"The financial statements articulate," Mo said, echoing a term he'd introduced months ago. "Just like different maps of the same terrain. Topographic, political, climate... each reveal different features but represent the same landscape."

Greg's expression brightened with understanding. "And it's not just the statements. It's how financial decisions connect to everything else. Operations, customer relationships, employee management, growth strategy."

"Now you're really getting it." Mo smiled. "Finance isn't a department or a function, it's the language of business decisions. When you're fluent in that language, you make better decisions in every area."

They finished eating, and Mo suggested a walk. The café sat atop a small hill overlooking the city, with a walking path that circled a nearby park. The morning was crisp but pleasant, perfect for reflection.

"I've been thinking about our journey this past year," Mo said as they walked. "We started with the mechanics: how to read and use financial statements. Then we explored applications: timing, scaling, crisis management. Finally, we examined the strategic view: long-term planning and multiple horizons."

"Like climbing a mountain," Greg observed. "First you learn the equipment, then how to navigate different terrain, and finally how to choose which peaks to summit."

"Apt metaphor." Mo said, not masking his approval. "And now comes the most important phase: the return journey."

"What do you mean?"

"In mountaineering, reaching the summit is only half the journey. The return trip is where many experienced climbers face their greatest challenges." Mo paused at a viewpoint overlooking the city. "In business, applying what you've learned consistently over time—through changing conditions and inevitable setbacks—that's the return journey."

Greg ran his hand through his hair thoughtfully. "So we're not really finishing our lessons."

"We're transitioning from instruction to implementation." Mo turned to face him. "I can't teach you anything more valuable than what you'll learn by applying these principles yourself, day after day, year after year."

They continued walking, passing a playground where early-rising families had brought children to play. Mo watched them with a thoughtful expression.

"You know, financial literacy isn't taught in most schools," he observed. "Most people learn it the hard way, through costly mistakes and missed opportunities. Or they never learn it at all, living financially-reactive lives rather than proactive ones."

"I was headed that way before you stepped in," Greg admitted.

"Which brings me to an important question." Mo stopped, his expression serious. "What will you do with this knowledge?"

"Grow my business, obviously."

"Beyond that." Mo's gaze was steady. "Knowledge creates responsibility. Financial literacy is too valuable, and too rare, to keep to yourself."

Greg understood the implication. "You think I should teach others what I've learned."

"In time, yes. Not immediately. You need to deepen your mastery through practice. But eventually." Mo resumed walking. "The best way to honor a gift is to pass it on."

They completed their circuit of the park, returning to the café parking lot. Mo leaned against his truck.

"I have something for you," he said, reaching into the vehicle. He pulled out a package wrapped in simple brown paper.

Greg accepted it, surprised by its weight. Unwrapping it revealed a handsome leather-bound ledger, its cover embossed with a mountain peak design. Inside were blank pages of high-quality paper, structured for financial recordkeeping but unmarked.

"It's beautiful," Greg said, running his hand over the cover, fondly remembering Mo's well-worn version.

"My father gave me something similar when I started my first business," Mo explained. "I've kept every important financial decision, insight, and lesson in ledgers like this one. More valuable than any digital record because they capture not just what happened, but what I learned from it."

Greg opened to the first page, finding a handwritten inscription:

Financial statements tell a company's story in numbers. Make yours a story worth telling. - Mo

"Thank you," Greg said, genuinely moved. "For this, and for everything this year."

"You did the work," Mo replied. "I just provided direction."

They said their goodbyes, but as Greg turned to leave, Mo called after him.

"One last thing, Greggo. The most important financial insight I've ever discovered."

Greg turned back, instinctively reaching for his notebook.

Mo smiled. "You don't need to write this one down. Just remember it: Money is never the ultimate destination; it's just fuel for the journey toward what truly matters."

On impulse that evening, Greg picked up his phone and called Mo.

"Hey, Uncle Mo. Are you free tomorrow for a ride?"

"For you? Always," Mo replied. "What's the occasion?"

"Just feeling reflective. Thought we could revisit Prospect Avenue."

The next afternoon, they were pedaling up the same hill where their lessons had begun a year ago. Greg rode his old Schwinn rather than borrowing Mo's bike, a choice that felt symbolically right for the day.

"So," Mo said as they climbed steadily, "what prompted this nostalgic journey?"

Greg shifted gears smoothly, finding a comfortable rhythm. "I've been thinking about everything I've learned this year. How different my understanding is now compared to when we started."

"How so?" Mo asked, a smile in his voice.

"At first, I just wanted to know enough to not mess up my lawn business," Greg explained. "Now I see financial statements as stories about what matters and where we're heading. I'm reading the business landscape in a completely different way."

They reached the summit and stopped at the same bench where they'd rested during their first lesson. The view of the town spread below them, but now Greg saw it differently. He saw not just houses and businesses, but a landscape of interconnected financial flows, challenges, and opportunities.

"You've come a long way," Mo observed, seeing Greg's contemplative expression. "From asking basic questions to seeing the bigger picture."

"I'm starting to think about what's next," Greg admitted. "Not just growing the lawn business, but maybe someday helping others the way you've helped me."

"Nobody ever feels ready for that step," Mo replied. "I certainly didn't when I started mentoring young entrepreneurs after selling my business."

"You never told me about that," Greg said, surprised.

Mo shrugged. "Small business incubator downtown. I volunteer there twice a month, helping startups with their financial strategies." He smiled. "I've been using the same bicycle metaphors with them for years. They work."

They sat in comfortable silence for a moment, watching the sunset paint the sky.

"There's something powerful about helping someone see their business through a new lens," Greg pondered. "Showing them patterns and possibilities they couldn't see before."

"That's how knowledge truly becomes yours," Mo responded. "You don't really own an idea until you can give it away."

Greg thought about the leather ledger Mo had given him, now waiting to be filled with insights not just about his own business, but perhaps someday about helping others.

"I'm not planning to become a financial consultant," Greg clarified. "The lawn business is still my focus. But maybe there's room for both. Building my company and occasionally helping other small business owners understand what took me so long to learn."

"The best journeys usually have multiple destinations," Mo said, standing up. "Ready to head back down?"

As they began the descent, Greg found himself riding with a confidence that hadn't existed a year ago, reading the terrain ahead, anticipating turns, adjusting his speed with precision. His understanding of business had evolved in the same way, from novice uncertainty to a more intuitive grasp of the underlying patterns.

"One last race to the bottom?" Mo challenged with a grin.

"You're on," Greg replied, leaning into the first turn.

They picked up speed, the wind rushing past as gravity pulled them down the hill he'd struggled to climb that first day. Greg found himself laughing, not from the thrill of the descent but from the realization of how far he'd come—in business, in understanding, and in his relationship with Mo.

After Jason left, Greg opened his leather ledger and made a new entry, not about his own business this time, but about what he'd observed in helping someone else. The technical issues were familiar, but the human element—the mix of family obligation, pride, and uncertainty Jason felt about the inherited store—added layers of complexity to the financial decisions.

As he'd grown accustomed to doing, Greg wrote in his journal:

Financial knowledge without empathy is just mathematics. The human context gives the numbers meaning.

He closed the ledger, thinking about Mo's final insight: money as fuel, not destination. In helping Jason, he'd glimpsed what that truly meant. He saw how financial literacy could empower someone to preserve not just a business, but a family legacy.

His phone rang. Mo's name appeared on the screen.

"Perfect timing," Greg answered. "I was just thinking about you."

"Good thoughts, I hope."

"The best. I just finished meeting with a new client, young guy who inherited his grandfather's hardware store. Found myself channeling your teaching methods to explain cash flow concepts."

Mo chuckled. "The return journey begins. How did it feel?"

"Surprisingly fulfilling," Greg admitted. "Different from lawn care work, but somehow complementary."

"That's how it starts," Mo said, his voice warm with approval. "One conversation, one insight shared, one person helped. Before you know it, you've become a guide for others, just as others guided you."

They talked for a while longer about Greg's business developments and Mo's latest projects with his nonprofit work. As they were about to hang up, Greg had a sudden thought.

"Hey, Uncle Mo. That LeMond story you told me when we first started, about seeing the Tour de France win coming and positioning your bike shop to capitalize on it. There was more to that story, wasn't there?"

A brief silence followed, then Mo's soft laugh. "Clever boy. Yes, there was more. Perhaps someday I'll tell you the full version. But for now, let's just say I had unique insights into that particular competitor's potential."

"I knew it! You weren't just a fan, were you?"

"Everyone has chapters in their story that aren't immediately visible on their personal P&L," Mo replied cryptically. "The full narrative emerges over time, for those paying attention."

After they hung up, Greg found himself thinking about Mo's journey from bike shop owner to landscaping entrepreneur to mentor and nonprofit leader. The visible achievements were impressive enough, but Greg suspected the unseen dimensions of Mo's story held even richer lessons.

Perhaps that was the ultimate insight from their year of financial education: Behind every set of numbers is a human story. Balance sheets balance. Cash flows circulate. And P&Ls track. But these are just structured reflections of human decisions, aspirations, and values.

Greg opened the leather ledger one more time, turning to a fresh page. At the top, he wrote:

Chapter Two: Becoming a Guide.

Below that, he began noting ideas for how he might formalize what he was already beginning to do, helping others understand the financial principles that had transformed his own business journey.

Not immediately, as Mo had cautioned. He still had much to learn through direct application. But eventually, perhaps in a year or two, he could develop workshops for local small business owners, or mentor young entrepreneurs, or even write about his experiences.

The ledger's remaining blank pages represented not just his business's future, but the potential to influence others' journeys as well. Like Mo, he could help translate the language of finance into accessible wisdom that empowered better decisions.

As Greg closed the ledger, he reflected on how far he'd come from that first day in Mo's garage. He had sought advice about starting a lawn care business but received something far more valuable: a framework for understanding how money moves through businesses and lives, creating possibilities and illuminating paths forward.

The financial statements he'd learned to read and create were more than compliance documents or business tools. They were maps for the journey ahead, a journey he now felt equipped to navigate with confidence, clarity, and an appreciation for both the direct route and the scenic detours along the way.

And perhaps most valuably, he'd discovered that the most fulfilling application of financial knowledge wasn't just in building personal wealth, but in helping others find their own path through the seemingly intimidating terrain of business finance.

The return journey wasn't an ending but a beginning, a chance to transform what he'd learned into impact that extended beyond his own balance sheet. Cash might flow in cycles, but knowledge and wisdom, once shared, continued flowing outward, creating value that no financial statement could fully capture.

APPENDIX

FROM GREG'S LEATHER-BOUND LEDGER

The following pages were transcribed from Greg's leather-bound ledger, the same one Mo gave him on their one-year anniversary. These notes represent Greg's personal compilation of Uncle Mo's wisdom, methods, and practical applications.

Uncle Mo's Greatest Hits

Wisdom I never want to forget, organized by topic

On Cash Flow Fundamentals

Cash flow is the lifeblood of your business. Without it, you might as well be pedaling a bike with a flat tire. You can push hard, but you won't get far.

Out here, timing matters more than total. You can make a million dollars on paper and still go bankrupt waiting for the money to arrive.

First lesson: figure out how long you can go without getting paid. Your 'runway,' so to speak. Most people think too much about profit and not enough about timing.

Better to be prepared with an imperfect plan than perfectly unprepared!

Build a business that can weather the terrain ahead, not just the terrain you can see.

On Financial Statements

Profit and Loss (P&L) Statement

The P&L tells you how fast you're moving. It's like a video—showing movement over time.

The numbers tell you what happened. The notes tell you why.

The P&L is your business dashboard. It tells you if you need to raise prices, cut costs, or find more clients.

The P&L can lie to you. It shows you earned $5,000 this month but doesn't tell you that $3,000 of it hasn't been paid yet.

The P&L shows results, not effort. Remember that when things get tough.

Balance Sheet

The Balance Sheet is the pause button. One precise moment, frozen.

Your Balance Sheet tells you where your weight is distributed. Too much debt? You'll topple forward. Not enough liquid assets? You can't absorb impacts.

The total asset value doesn't always change, but the composition of those assets does. Asset composition matters as much as total value.

Cash might be king, but a strong Balance Sheet is what lets you sleep at night.

Cash Flow Statement

The Cash Flow Statement is where it all comes together. It shows how your P&L performance translates into actual cash movement on your Balance Sheet.

Cash flow is where the P&L meets the Balance Sheet. It translates profit into actual money movement. It's like looking at the balance sheet over time.

Cash is oxygen for a business. The flow sometimes matters even more than the amount.

On Financial Statements Working Together

They articulate with each other. They tell the same story from different angles.

Think of it this way: The P&L shows what you earned. The Balance Sheet shows what you have. The Cash Flow Statement shows what moved. Together, they tell the complete story.

On Business Growth

Growth for growth's sake is a trap. Especially for small businesses.

There are four types of business growth: vertical, horizontal, process, and financial. Each affects your cash flow differently.

Scale in stages, ensuring each stage generates cash before committing to the next.

Many entrepreneurs try to scale a flawed model and wonder why they struggle.

The most dangerous point in scaling is when you've committed to the higher fixed costs but haven't yet generated the additional revenue to support them.

The skills that got you here won't get you there. Solo success requires technical excellence. Scaling requires systems thinking and leadership.

Never forget—growth consumes cash. The faster you grow, the more working capital you need.

On Cash Flow Timing

Timing – it isn't just about having enough money—it's about having it when you need it.

In business, you need to synchronize three timeframes—operational cycle, customer payment cycle, and supplier payment cycle. When they're aligned, cash flows smoothly.

The right resource at the wrong time is still the wrong resource.

Sometimes you need to push hard and grow quickly. Other times, slowing down and conserving resources is the smarter move.

On Crisis Management

The question isn't if storms will come, but how you'll handle them when they do.

In a crisis, accelerate all inflows and delay all outflows—ethically and without damaging relationships.

Not all parts of your business have equal value during a crisis. Protect from the inside out.

In a true crisis, <u>your relationships become your most valuable currency</u>.

<u>Crisis reveals character</u>, both personal and organizational. How you respond when things are at their worst defines you more clearly than all your actions when things are going well.

The businesses that emerge strongest from crises are those that stay true to their core values while being flexible about almost everything else.

<u>Paradox</u>: When you're thoroughly prepared for a crisis, you're less likely to experience one. The very act of planning reduces your vulnerability.

In crisis, preserve cash, protect relationships, and remember that <u>how you respond defines who you are</u>.

On Long-Term Planning

The balance sheet and cash flow management we've discussed—those are tactical tools. Essential for day-to-day operations and near-term planning. But <u>long-term success requires strategic thinking</u> that goes beyond financial statements.

Most business owners obsess over goals but underinvest in systems. The irony is that systems are far more important for long-term success.

Poor businesses sacrifice long-term value for short-term gain. Average businesses balance the two. <u>Great businesses find strategies that serve both simultaneously</u>.

understanding that success isn't about where you are now, but which direction you're moving and at what speed.

The scenic route takes longer but reveals better destinations.

The <u>value of a forecast</u> isn't in creating a perfect roadmap to a predetermined destination. It's in <u>developing the strategic thinking muscles</u> that let you navigate effectively regardless of how the landscape changes.

On Business and Life

<u>Finance</u> isn't a department or a function—<u>it's the language of business</u> decisions. When you're fluent in that language, you make better decisions in every area.

Financial literacy changes your perspective. It's like getting glasses after years of blurry vision.

<u>Accounting tells you what happened. Finance helps you decide what to do next</u>. That's the art part of the science.

Money is never the ultimate destination—it's just fuel for the journey toward what truly matters.

<u>Financial knowledge without empathy is just mathematics</u>. The human context gives the numbers meaning.

The Mo Methods (Frameworks I use in my business)

The Three Financial Statements Approach

How I apply this to my lawn business: I review all three statements monthly, checking that my P&L profits are actually showing up as increased cash and equity.

P&L Statement - Shows movement over time (like a video)

- What you earned and spent
- Where revenue came from
- Where expenses went
- Net result for a period

Balance Sheet - Shows position at a moment in timer (like a photograph or the pause button)

- What you own (assets)
- What you owe (liabilities)
- What's truly yours (equity)
- Strength and composition of resources

Cash Flow Statement - Shows actual money movement (Balance Sheet over time)

- How net income translates to cash
- Sources and uses of cash
- Operating, investing, and financing activities
- Net change in cash position

The Storm Protocol for Crisis Management

How I apply this to my lawn business: I created a specific Storm Protocol for weather disruptions, equipment failures, and potential loss of key clients. When we had three straight rain days last month, having this plan ready kept me from panicking.

<u>**Immediate Protection**</u> (First 24-48 hours)

- Preserve core cash reserves
- Communicate transparently with stakeholders
- Address immediate existential threats

<u>Damage Assessment</u> (Days 3-7)

- Quantify exact impacts
- Identify affected business areas
- Distinguish between temporary and permanent damage

<u>Strategic Reconstruction</u>

- Strengthen obvious vulnerabilities
- Preserve and expand core strengths
- Strategically abandon unsustainable areas

The Three Cash Flow Strategies for Crisis

How I apply this to my lawn business: I implemented the Cash Acceleration Strategy during the spring rains by offering a 5% discount for advance payments on seasonal contracts, which brought in much-needed cash during a slow period.

Cash Acceleration Strategy

- Accelerate all inflows (offer discounts for immediate payment)
- Delay all outflows (extend payables where possible)
- Convert inventory or unused assets to cash

Segmented Preservation

- Identify essential operations (inner circle)
- Identify important but flexible components (middle circle)
- Identify non-essential elements (outer circle)
- Protect from the inside out

Relationship Banking (depositing in the relational bank)

- Build relationships before you need them
- Pay suppliers early when you can
- Deliver extra value to clients occasionally
- Support employees during personal challenges
- Maintain perfect communication with lenders

The Four Types of Business Growth

How I apply this to my lawn business: I'm currently focused on vertical growth—adding edge trimming and basic hedge services for existing clients—because it has the best cash flow profile for my current stage.

Vertical Growth

- Serving same customers with more services/products
- Leverages existing relationships
- Moderate cash flow impact
- Requires new skills and inventory

Horizontal Growth

- Expanding core service to more customers
- Replicates existing model
- Significant cash flow impact
- Requires similar upfront costs for each new customer/location

Process Growth

- Improving efficiency of existing operations
- Heavy upfront cash investment
- Delayed returns
- Permanently improved margins once absorbed

Financial Growth

- Improving margins, cash flow, returns without selling more
- Using pricing strategies, payment terms, inventory management
- Variable cash flow impact
- Often most capital-efficient

The Three Cash Flow Timing Strategies

How I apply this to my lawn business: I've implemented the Synchronization strategy by scheduling my client invoicing on Mondays and my supplier payments on Fridays, ensuring I have cash in hand before major outflows.

Negotiation

- Get some clients to pay half upfront
- Extend supplier payment terms
- Align payment schedules with cash needs

Staggering

- Create rolling replacement schedules for equipment
- Add staff gradually rather than all at once
- Spread major expenditures across time

Synchronization

- Align billing cycles with payroll cycles
- Schedule supplier payments for days after client payments typically arrive
- Coordinate timing of cash inflows and outflows

The Three Horizons Planning Framework

How I apply this to my lawn business: My First Horizon plan includes adding edging services and one part-time employee; Second Horizon focuses on equipment upgrades and possible commercial clients; Third Horizon envisions a sustainable landscape management business with educational components.

First Horizon (Next 12 months)

- Specific, actionable steps
- Clear metrics and cash flow projections
- Tactical improvements

Second Horizon (1-3 years)

- Strategic initiatives
- Capability development
- Market positioning
- Directional rather than tactical

Third Horizon (3-10 years)

- Values and impact
- Business's role in your life
- Place in the market
- Legacy considerations

ACKNOWLEDGEMENTS

THIS BOOK EXISTS because of **Adam's** suggestion to turn an insight into a parable. It began as a casual telephone conversation during his commute to a client. "Your explanations always use stories. Why not write the whole thing that way?" His rhetorical question planted the seed that blossomed into something larger than I imagined. That spark kept me going through many painful drafts. Drafts that felt like climbing Mountain View Road in the wrong gear! Thank you, my friend, for seeing possibilities I hadn't yet realized.

To **Uncle Nestor**, who taught me financial—and life—principles, not through lectures but through lived example. I am grateful for his willingness to ask the hard questions and then push back when my answers were weak. His ability to distill complex concepts into practical wisdom while *jumping blacks* in Colorado formed the blueprint for Uncle Mo. Though he didn't live to see this book completed, his fingerprints are on every page. I hope this work reflects even a fraction of what I learned from you.

To **Dan**, whose mentorship began in childhood and remained through every critical juncture in my professional life. He challenged my assumptions, refined my thinking, and demonstrated that true leadership means serving and elevating others. The financial frameworks we developed together have guided countless business decisions, and now, reimagined through cycling metaphors, they form the backbone of this book. His impact remains immeasurable, and I will continue to acknowledge his influence every chance I get.

To **Pam**, my steadfast companion through late nights of writing and rewriting, who endured countless impromptu conversations about subjects that *could not have been exciting* for you. Your unwavering support through all my writing endeavors. I wouldn't be doing this without you.

To my **early readers**, those brave souls who engaged with rough drafts and provided the feedback that shaped this final version. Your insights helped me find the balance between technical accuracy and narrative engagement.

To **small business owners everywhere**, the unsung heroes of our economy and communities. The risk-takers working from kitchen tables and home offices long after their kids are in bed. The problem-solvers who see opportunity where others see obstacles. The ones cranking on the pedals even when the trail ahead seems impossibly steep.

And especially to **nonprofit leaders everywhere,** who navigate the same financial challenges while stretching limited resources to meet unlimited needs, you accomplish the extraordinary with ordinary budgets, balancing mission and margin with grace and determination. Your commitment to creating positive change while maintaining financial sustainability is a balancing act that rarely receives the recognition it deserves. This book is for all of you. May it provide not just techniques, but the encouragement to keep pedaling, one revolution at a time.

Finally, I'd like to thank **my Lord and Savior, Jesus Christ**. *In moments of clarity and confusion alike, I lean daily on Your guidance. Through You, I find purpose in sharing what I've learned. And apart from You, I can do nothing.*

ABOUT THE AUTHOR

DELTON DE ARMAS WORKS as a business strategist, fractional executive, and financial consultant, helping entrepreneurs, small business owners, and nonprofit leaders master their numbers. With a background in accounting, finance, and operations, he has spent years guiding organizations through financial complexities, transforming abstract concepts into actionable strategies.

Beyond the spreadsheets, Delton tells stories, mentors leaders, and solves problems, believing financial literacy goes beyond numbers; it creates freedom, stability, and opportunity. Through writing, speaking, and consulting, he equips and empowers others to make their own shift from survival to sustainable success.

When not helping organizations thrive, he cycles, writes songs, and explores the scenic routes of both business and life. He lives in Ocala, Florida, with his wife, Pam.

www.ingramcontent.com/pod-product-compliance
Lightning Source LLC
Chambersburg PA
CBHW030832090426
42737CB00009B/974